TURGOT
on Progress, Sociology and Economics

Cambridge Studies in the History and Theory of Politics

EDITORS

MAURICE COWLING   J. G. A. POCOCK

G. R. ELTON   J. R. POLE

E. KEDOURIE   WALTER ULLMANN

For a complete list of books in this series see page 186

TURGOT
on Progress, Sociology and Economics

A Philosophical Review of the Successive Advances of the Human Mind
On Universal History
Reflections on the Formation and the Distribution of Wealth

Translated, edited and with an introduction by
RONALD L. MEEK
TYLER PROFESSOR OF ECONOMICS
UNIVERSITY OF LEICESTER

CAMBRIDGE
AT THE UNIVERSITY PRESS 1973

PUBLISHED BY THE SYNDICS OF THE CAMBRIDGE UNIVERSITY PRESS
BENTLEY HOUSE, 200 EUSTON ROAD, LONDON, NW1 2BD
AMERICAN BRANCH: 32 EAST 57TH STREET, NEW YORK, N.Y. 10022

© CAMBRIDGE UNIVERSITY PRESS 1973

LIBRARY OF CONGRESS CATALOGUE CARD NUMBER: 72-83594

ISBN: 0 521 08698 1

PRINTED IN GREAT BRITAIN BY
WESTERN PRINTING SERVICES LIMITED, BRISTOL

Contents

Acknowledgements

I am extremely grateful to Dr P. D. Groenewegen, of the University of Sydney, who has put his extensive knowledge of Turgot's economic work at my disposal on several occasions during the preparation of this book. I am also grateful to Columbia University for supplying me with the microfilm mentioned on p. 38.

R.L.M.

Introduction

There are minds to whom nature has given a memory which is capable of
assembling together a large number of pieces of knowledge, a power
of exact reasoning which is capable of comparing them and arranging them
in a manner which puts them in their full light, but to whom at the same
time she has denied that fire of genius which invents and which opens
up new roads for itself. Created to unite past discoveries under one point
of view, to clarify and even to perfect them, if they are not torches
which shine with their own light, they are diamonds which brilliantly reflect
a borrowed light, but which total darkness would confound with the
meanest stones.

Turgot, *Philosophical Review*

(*a*) TURGOT'S LIFE, AND THE EDITIONS OF HIS WORKS

Turgot was fond of this comparison between 'torches which shine with
their own light' and 'diamonds which brilliantly reflect a borrowed light'.
The particular version quoted above is from the discourse which he read
at the *Maison de Sorbonne* in December 1750.[1] But we find it earlier than
this, in a set of notes on 'The Causes of the Progress and Decline of the
Sciences and the Arts' which he apparently wrote in 1748;[2] and later than
this, in almost the same form, in his notes on 'Universal History' which
probably date from 1751.[3] Whether he had himself in mind when he
wrote this passage we do not know, but the description fits him so
admirably that this may not be beyond the bounds of possibility.

Certainly, at any rate, Turgot set out from the beginning with the
conscious intention of becoming a polymath rather than a specialist in one
particular field of enquiry. There is extant an extraordinary 'List of Works
to be Written' which he apparently prepared at the outset of his career.[4]
It begins with '*The Barmecides*, a tragedy' and ends with '*On luxury*,

---

[1] Translated below, pp. 41–59. The passage appears on p. 51.
[2] *Œuvres de Turgot et documents le concernant*, ed. G. Schelle (Paris, 1913–23), Vol. I,
pp. 116–42. The passage appears on pp. 132–3. Schelle's edition of the *Œuvres* will
henceforth be referred to simply as 'Schelle'.
[3] Translated below, pp. 61–118. The passage appears on p. 115.
[4] Schelle, I, pp. 115–16.

I

political reflections'; and in between these are forty-eight others, including works on universal history, the origin of languages, love and marriage,
political geography, natural theology, morality, and economics, as well as
numerous translations from foreign languages, literary works, and
treatises on scientific subjects. Even making allowances for the natural
ebullience and optimism of an extremely gifted and precocious young
man, this list of subjects is remarkable; but what is even more remarkable
is the fact that Turgot managed, during his short life of only fifty-four
years (1727–81), to make some kind of contribution to so many of them,
or at least to retain an active and intelligent interest in them.

Turgot came of an old and fairly well-placed noble Norman family,
with a longish record of administrative service. As a third son he was
destined for the Church, and in 1749, after brilliantly sustaining his thesis
for the degree of Bachelor of Theology, he was admitted to the *Maison de
Sorbonne*, an annex of the theological faculty of the University of Paris,
to read for his *license*. He was soon elected *prieur*, a largely honorary
office which involved presiding over assemblies of theological students
and delivering on certain occasions a discourse in Latin. The second of
the two discourses which Turgot delivered in this capacity (on 11 December 1750) – *A Philosophical Review of the Successive Advances of the Human
Mind* – is the first of the three texts translated in the present volume. The
second text translated here – *On Universal History* – also probably dates
from the close of his Sorbonne period, or at any rate shortly thereafter.

Early in 1751, Turgot announced his decision to abandon the ecclesiastical career upon which he had embarked, and to enter instead the service
of the Crown. From 1752 to 1761 he held various offices of a judicial-
cum-administrative character, being appointed *Maître des Requêtes* in
1753. During this period he wrote five articles for the *Encyclopedia*
(*Étymologie*, *Existence*, and *Expansibilité* in 1756; *Foire* and *Fondation* in
1757), and began taking a more profound interest in economics. His most
important work in the latter field during this period was the *Éloge* which
he wrote in 1759 on the occasion of the death of his friend Vincent de
Gournay,[1] whom he had earlier accompanied on several official tours of
inspection of trade and manufactures in a number of French provinces.

In August 1761 Turgot was appointed *Intendant* of the *généralité* of
Limoges, a post which he held with great distinction for the next thirteen
years. The *généralité* concerned was quite a large one, including as it did
most of the two provinces of Limousin and Angoumois together with
certain other areas; and Turgot's task as *Intendant* was to act there as

[1] See below, pp. 15–16.

general administrator and representative of the central authority. From
the economic point of view the *généralité* was one of the poorest and least
developed in France, and Turgot flung himself with great zeal and energy
into the task of instituting various much-needed reforms. In spite of his
preoccupation with administrative duties, this period was the most fruitful of his life so far as his output of economic writings was concerned. It
saw (*inter alia*) his *mémoires* on mines and quarries (1764) and on the loan
of money (1770); his observations on the *mémoires* of Graslin and Saint-
Péravy (1767); his article on 'Value and Money' (*c.* 1769); his letters to
Terray on the corn trade (1770); and, above all, his *Reflections on the
Formation and the Distribution of Wealth*, which is the third piece translated in the present volume.

In 1774, after a brief period as Minister of Marine, Turgot was appointed to the high office of *Contrôleur Général des Finances*, but retained
this post for less than two years. The story of his short ministry is a
fascinating one, and has been the subject of intense debate among historians from that day to this. After his fall from power in 1776 he went
into retirement, dying of gout – the family disease – on 18 March 1781.

Not very many of Turgot's writings were 'published' – at any rate in
the ordinary sense of that word – during his lifetime. Some appeared
anonymously in one form or another in periodicals; copies of some (e.g.
the *Philosophical Review* and the *Reflections*) were distributed among
selected recipients; but a large number took the form of letters, private
memoranda, papers addressed to his superiors, preambles to edicts, etc.
It was not until 1808–11 that a collected edition of his works appeared,
under the editorship of Du Pont de Nemours.[1] Much has been written
about Du Pont's low standards of editorship, and especially about his
habit of 'correcting' works (including Turgot's) which came to him for
publication; and it is indeed difficult to forgive him for some of his
actions.[2] But it should not be forgotten that we owe a considerable debt
of gratitude to Du Pont: without his labours we would have known much
less about Turgot than we in fact do know today, and several important
writings – including *On Universal History* – might well have been lost for
ever.

A second edition of the *Œuvres*, edited by Daire and Dussard, appeared
in 1844, but it was not until 1913–23, when the five monumental volumes

[1] *Œuvres de M*^r*. Turgot, Ministre d'État* (Paris, 1808–11), 9 volumes. Du Pont's edition
of the *Œuvres* will henceforth be referred to simply as 'Du Pont'.
[2] Particularly his inclusion in the *Œuvres* of the text of the *Reflections* which had appeared
originally in *Éphémérides*, instead of that of the amended offprint which Turgot had
subsequently authorised (see below, pp. 37–9).

of Schelle's *Œuvres de Turgot et documents le concernant* were published, that the world was given anything which really deserved the title of a definitive edition. Schelle was able to include a large amount of new material, and he took some care to eradicate Du Pont's 'corrections'. In a number of cases, however, he was unable to find the originals of documents which Du Pont had published, so that he could do no more than republish Du Pont's text.

The translation of the *Philosophical Review* which appears below has been made from the version in Schelle's edition.[1] The translation of *On Universal History*, however, has been made from the version in Du Pont's edition.[2] This is one of the cases just mentioned where Schelle was unable to find the original manuscript, and since his text differs from that of Du Pont in certain respects (paragraphing, emphases, etc.) I have thought it proper to go back to Du Pont.[3] It is quite possible that Du Pont's text embodies 'corrections', but it is all that we have. So far as the translation of the *Reflections* is concerned, for reasons spelt out in Appendix B to this introduction I have used neither Du Pont nor Schelle, but a separate edition of the *Reflections* apparently published in 1788.

(b) THE 'PHILOSOPHICAL REVIEW' AND 'ON UNIVERSAL HISTORY'

Turgot's notes, mentioned above, on 'The Causes of the Progress and Decline of the Sciences and the Arts',[4] were probably written in 1748, at any rate if we are to judge from a marginal note referring to a prize to be offered early in 1749 by the Academy of Soissons for a discourse on this subject. It is clear from these fragmentary but quite extensive notes that many of the views which Turgot was later to express in the *Philosophical Review* and *On Universal History* were already formed before he entered the Sorbonne: the notes obviously constituted part of the raw material upon which he drew when he was writing these two pieces. A number of the more picturesque analogies used in the latter are to be found already in the notes; there are distinct traces of the 'materialist' approach which

---

[1] Schelle, I, pp. 214–35; cf. Du Pont, II, pp. 52–92.

[2] Du Pont, II, pp. 209–328. Translations of Du Pont's foreword and concluding remarks have been added. Cf. Schelle, I, pp. 275–323.

[3] Another reason for using Du Pont rather than Schelle on this occasion is that the version published by Schelle omits a number of passages which are substantially duplicated in the 1748 notes on 'The Causes of the Progress and Decline of the Sciences and the Arts'.

[4] Schelle, I, pp. 116–42.

he was later to employ much more extensively; the critique of Montesquieu's theory of the influence of climate which appears in *On Universal History*[1] is present in the notes in embryo;[2] and there, too, is the famous prophecy about the coming revolt of the American colonies.[3] But three major unifying constituents of the later works are still lacking. First, although there is a passing reference to Locke's notion that 'all our ideas come to us from the senses',[4] there is no indication of the important role which this notion was later to play in Turgot's thinking. Second, although the notes contain several references to different arts and sciences being 'perfected', no general doctrine of perfectibility is explicitly stated. And third, there is no indication of the stadial theory of socio-economic development which was to become part of the framework of *On Universal History*.

In a critique which Turgot wrote in March 1750 of a book on the origin of languages by Maupertuis,[5] however, the sensationalist theory of Locke pervades the whole, and, even more important, the outlines of a stadial theory of the development of early society are fairly clearly delineated. 'Thence arose the different languages', Turgot writes, 'according to whether the people were hunters, shepherds, or husbandmen...The hunter would have few words, very vivid, not closely linked together, and progress would be slow; the shepherd, with his peaceful life, would construct a gentler and more refined language; the husbandman, one that was colder and more coherent.'[6] The general idea implied here – that early society proceeds naturally and successively through the hunting, pastoral, and agricultural stages, each with its own 'superstructure' of languages, laws, customs, etc. – was destined to be of great importance, not only for Turgot's own work, but also for the emergence and development of social science as a whole in the eighteenth century.[7]

It is possible that the inspiration for this seminal idea came to Turgot from Montesquieu. At the end of Book I of *L'Esprit des Lois*, Montesquieu says that the laws ought to be related to (*inter alia*) 'the principal occupation of the natives, whether husbandmen, huntsmen, or shepherds';[8]

---

[1] Below, pp. 89–90.
[2] Schelle, I, pp. 139–40. Montesquieu's *L'Esprit des Lois* appeared in 1748, the same year as that from which the notes apparently date.
[3] Schelle, I, p. 141.
[4] Schelle, I, p. 140.
[5] Schelle, I, pp. 157–79; cf. Du Pont, II, pp. 102–64.
[6] Schelle, I, p. 172; cf. Du Pont, II, p. 143.
[7] Cf. my article 'Smith, Turgot, and the "Four Stages" Theory' (*The History of Political Economy*, Vol. III, no. 1, Spring 1971, pp. 9–27).
[8] *The Spirit of the Laws* (Hafner Library of Classics, New York, 1949), p. 6.

and in Book XVIII ('Of Laws in the Relation they Bear to the Nature of the Soil') we find the following statement:

The laws have a very great relation to the manner in which the several nations procure their subsistence. There should be a code of laws of a much larger extent for a nation attached to trade and navigation than for people who are content with cultivating the earth. There should be a much greater for the latter than for those who subsist by their flocks and herds. There must be a still greater for these than for such as live by hunting.[1]

These statements, and some of the rather haphazard comments which follow,[2] may well have seized Turgot's imagination. But it must be emphasised that the clarity with which Turgot expressed the idea, the way in which he refined and developed it, and the uses to which he put it, mark him and not Montesquieu out as the one who really deserves the name of innovator.

On 3 July 1750, in his capacity as *prieur*, Turgot gave the first of his two discourses at the Sorbonne, under the title *The Advantages which the Establishment of Christianity has Procured for the Human Race*.[3] This rather over-eloquent piece is usually compared unfavourably with his second discourse of 11 December 1750 – the famous *Philosophical Review of the Successive Advances of the Human Mind* which is translated below. But the 3 July discourse is rather more significant than it is usually made out to be. In it, Turgot sets out to show how the doctrines of Christianity have helped to temper human passions, to perfect governments, and to make men better and happier. He begins by considering the effects of the Christian religion on men considered in themselves, concentrating here on such matters as the preservation of classical literature by the monks, the abolition of cruel customs such as the exposure of children, and, generally, the way in which Christianity has improved morals and manners and made men more humane. He then goes on, in the second and more interesting part of the discourse, 'to examine the progress of the art of government, and to show how Christianity has contributed to it'.[4] After a diatribe against great legislators, whose laws have a tendency to 'acquire a fatal immutability', he goes on to say this:

More happy are the nations whose laws have not been established by such great geniuses; they are at any rate perfected, although slowly and through a thousand detours, without principles, without perspectives, without a fixed plan; chance and circumstances have often led to wiser laws than have the researches and efforts of the human mind; an abuse which had been observed would give rise

[1] *Ibid.* p. 275.　　[2] *Ibid.* pp. 275–6, and cf. also pp. 278–9.
[3] Schelle, I, pp. 194–214; cf. Du Pont, II, pp. 17–51.
[4] Schelle, I, p. 206; cf. Du Pont, II, p. 38.

6

to a law; the abuse of that law would give rise to a second which modified it: by passing successively from one excess to the opposite excess, men little by little drew nearer to the happy medium.[1]

The important thing here, of course, is that it is not Christianity – nor, apparently, even the Deity – which produces 'these slow and successive advances'.[2] They occur, as it were, of themselves, and the role of Christianity is confined to eradicating injustices from the laws, spreading the idea that men – and nations – are brothers, and moderating the potentially despotic behaviour of monarchs.

In the discourse of 11 December 1750 these 'slow and successive advances' become in effect the main theme, and the part played by Christianity in the historical process of attaining perfection is summarised in a single paragraph (below, p. 53). And by the time one reaches this paragraph, with its question 'Holy religion, could it be that I should forget you?', one feels strongly not only that it could, but also that it almost was. Perhaps this is unfair to Turgot: it could be argued that the two discourses are in fact all of a piece – both are about progress and perfection, but the first deals with their sacred and the second with their secular aspects. There is an interesting parallel here with Bossuet's *Discours sur l'Histoire Universelle*, by which Turgot was greatly (if perversely) influenced:[3] in that book, a sacred history (mainly of the Jews) is followed by a completely separate secular history entitled 'The Empires'. Possibly what appears at first sight to be a conflict between Turgot's 3 July and 11 December discourses is merely another example of this kind of conscious and disciplined compartmentalisation. But it is rather more probable, I think, that the conflict was, at least in part, a real one, reflecting a mental struggle which was going on in his mind in the months immediately before he announced that he was abandoning his ecclesiastical career.[4]

'The whole human race, through alternate periods of rest and unrest, of weal and woe, goes on advancing, although at a slow pace, towards greater perfection' (below, p. 41). This is the main theme of Turgot's

---

[1] Schelle, I, p. 208. Du Pont omitted this paragraph from the text of the discourse published by him.

[2] *Ces progrès lents et successifs.*

[3] See below, pp. 28–9.

[4] See the interesting but unauthenticated anecdote in Du Pont, I, pp. 28–9, from which it would appear that at this time Turgot decided that it was impossible for him to go through life 'wearing a mask over his face'. But see also Condorcet's *Life of Turgot* (English translation, London, 1787), pp. 7–10 and 18, where the view is expressed that Turgot intended all the time to change his career as soon as he had finished his studies.

7

11 December discourse, in which the idea of progress which we particularly associate with the second half of the eighteenth century was put forward for the first time. The oratorical flights are sometimes tiresome, and the ritualistic passages at the end sound rather strangely in modern ears, but for all that the new message is clear enough. The keynote is sounded in the first two paragraphs. The 'succession of mankind', says Turgot, 'affords from age to age an ever-changing spectacle...All the ages are bound up with one another by a succession of causes and effects... Thus the human race, considered over the period since its origin, appears to the eye of a philosopher as one vast whole, which itself, like each individual, has its infancy and its advancement.' And this 'advancement', as the next paragraph makes clear, is 'towards greater perfection' (p. 41).

The aim of the discourse, then, is to illustrate this idea by indicating 'the main lines of the progress of the human mind', with particular reference to the development of the arts and sciences. The aim is, of course, over-ambitious, and it is often difficult to discern these 'main lines' beneath the wealth of detail and apostrophes. The unifying theme, however, is the Lockean notion that 'the senses constitute the unique source of our ideas' (below, p. 46, and cf. pp. 42 and 45), and the associated notion that 'the need perfects the tool' (p. 45). Turgot's argument seems to be that since all men have the same organs and senses, the spectacle of the same universe has always given them the same ideas; and since their needs and inclinations are broadly the same, they have always originated and perfected the same arts, and have proceeded through roughly the same stages of development from barbarism to refinement (pp. 42–3). But 'they do not all move forward at the same rate along the road which is marked out for them'. Turgot argues that 'circumstances' either encourage or discourage development, and it is the infinite variety of these 'circumstances' which brings about the manifest inequality in the progress of nations.

Given his general aim and this conceptual framework, then, Turgot is obliged to deal with two main questions – first, what exactly are these 'circumstances' which either increase or decrease the rate of progress; and second, why exactly is it that the general long-run tendency is in fact towards 'greater perfection' rather than towards, say, the reverse? Turgot does not clearly distinguish between these two questions, and his answer to the second and more important one is by no means fully worked out. The elements of his answer to it, however, may with a little effort be disentangled from the rest. First, the general process of the growth and development of societies is a *natural* process, comparable to the process of growth of the individual from infancy to adulthood, or that of the plant from seed to flower. Second, the main (although by no means the only) reasons why societies tend in the long run to develop towards 'greater perfection' are to be sought in the *economic* sphere. In the discourse, Turgot emphasises in this connection (*a*) the crucial importance of the emergence in the agricultural stage of development of a *social surplus*, which not only makes possible the development of 'towns, trade, the useful arts and accomplishments, the division of occupations', etc., but also facilitates the creation of a leisured class which 'bends all its strength to the cultivation of the arts' (below, p. 43); (*b*) the way in which the development of commerce is associated with the perfection of 'astronomy, navigation, and geography' (p. 47); (*c*) the important role of the towns – 'the centres of trade and the backbone of society' – in preventing the decline of the arts and sciences in periods of barbarism (p. 55); and (*d*) the way in which the 'mechanical arts' are preserved in times of general decline by the 'needs of life', and are developed in the long run merely by virtue of the fact that time passes (p. 55). To describe Turgot's argument in these terms is not, I think, to misrepresent it, although one is bound to look at it to some extent with the hindsight afforded by one's knowledge of his later work in this field.

All these ideas were clarified and developed further in *On Universal History*, which, together with its companion work *On Political Geography*, was written by Turgot (according to Du Pont) 'while he was at the Sorbonne, or shortly after he left it'.[1] Du Pont tells us that Turgot was planning a succession of three works, of which the first would have been Universal History, the second Political Geography, and the third a treatise on the Science of Government.[2] *On Political Geography* is interesting not only as further evidence of the extraordinary breadth and novelty of the young Turgot's interests and ideas, but also because it contains an important development of the 'three stages' theory. Turgot's notes consist essentially of a description of five 'political maps of the world',[3] the first of which would contain details of (*inter alia*) the following:

The successive changes in the manner of life of men, and the order in which they have followed one another: peoples who are shepherds, hunters, husbandmen.

[1] Du Pont, II, p. 165.
[2] Du Pont, *loc. cit.*
[3] *Mappemondes politiques.*

The causes which have been able to keep certain peoples for longer periods in the state of hunters, then shepherds. The differences which result from these three states, in relation to the number of men, to the movements of nations, to the greater or lesser degree of ease in surmounting the barriers by which nature has, so to speak, assigned to different societies their portion of the terrestrial globe, to communications, to the greater or lesser degree of ease with which peoples are intermingled.[1]

And the second 'political map of the world', similarly, would contain details of:

The first formation of governments among peoples who are savages, hunters, shepherds, husbandmen. The variations relative to these three manners of life.[2]

The 'three stages' theory which is expressed so clearly here by Turgot was, as I have already said, of great importance in the subsequent development of social science in the eighteenth century. Not only did it enable a plausible explanation of *differences* between societies to be given; but it also facilitated the formulation of a general theory of the *development* of society from lower to higher levels.

In *On Universal History*, Turgot makes a much more extensive use of the 'three stages' theory than in any of his earlier works. After a short introduction in which he describes the aim of 'universal history' as he understands it, he proceeds in the first of the two 'discourses' of which the work consists to consider the state of mankind immediately after the Flood. In the beginning, when men could devote themselves to nothing but obtaining their subsistence, they were primarily hunters, in much the same situation as the savages of America. But in countries where certain animals like oxen, sheep, and horses were to be found, 'the pastoral way of life' was introduced, resulting in an increase in wealth and a greater understanding of 'the idea of property'. Eventually, in fertile countries, pastoral peoples moved on to the state of agriculture, and as a result of the surplus which agriculture was able to generate there arose 'towns, trade, and all the useful arts and accomplishments', a leisured class, and so on. Within this conceptual framework, Turgot sets an account of wars and conquests among early peoples, the ways in which different nations were led to intermingle, and the overall effects of this intermingling.

Immediately after this section there is an important passage in which Turgot comes very close to the idea, later to be used so effectively by the

[1] Schelle, I, p. 259; cf. Du Pont, II, p. 174.
[2] Schelle, I, p. 260; cf. Du Pont, II, pp. 176–7.

members of the Scottish Historical School,[1] that the development of society is essentially a kind of unintended by-product of the conflict of human wills and actions which are often directed towards quite different ends. The passions of ambitious men, says Turgot, 'have led them on their way without their being aware of where they were going...They were, so to speak, the leading-strings with which nature and its Author guided the human race in its infancy...It is only through upheavals and ravages that nations have been extended, and that order and government have in the long run been perfected' (below, pp. 69–71).

> I seem to see [Turgot says] a huge army, every movement of which is directed by some mighty genius. When the military signals are given, when the trumpets sound tumultuously and the drums beat, whole squadrons of cavalry move off, the very horses are filled with a passion which has no aim, and each part of the army makes its way through the obstacles without knowing what may result from it: the leader alone sees the combined effect of all these different movements. Thus the passions have led to the multiplication of ideas, the extension of knowledge, and the perfection of the mind, in the absence of that reason whose day had not yet come and which would have been less powerful if its reign had arrived earlier. (pp. 69–70.)

One feels very strongly here that when Turgot speaks of the way in which, through this kind of mechanism, 'nature and its Author' guided the human race, it is nature rather than its Author to which he is mainly referring – that he is, in fact, feeling his way towards the idea that social development is due to the unfolding of certain immanent laws of history rather than to the conscious intervention of the Deity. This is a point on which I shall have something more to say later.[2]

In the remaining part of the first 'discourse', Turgot is concerned in the main with the development of different forms of government – as related in particular to the size and geographical situation of the nation concerned – and with the formation and conflicts of empires. These sections, although they contain many stimulating insights, are perhaps not as well organised as the earlier ones. A number of interesting themes are developed, however, notably the association of the 'spirit of equality' with the 'spirit of commerce' (below, p. 73), and the idea that knowledge and reason almost always, in one way or another, prevail over force (p. 75). And towards the end, when Turgot comes on to the subject of slavery, the 'three stages' idea is brought in once again as a conceptual framework (p. 81).

In the second 'discourse', Turgot is concerned mainly with progress in

[1] Cf. my *Economics and Ideology* (London, 1967), pp. 38–9.   [2] Below, pp. 27–9.

the arts and sciences. He begins with a fairly detailed account of the sensationalist psychology which, as we have already seen, was one of his great unifying themes, and, closely linked with this, a sketch of his theory of language (below, pp. 84–7). He then propounds a kind of 'law of uneven development' of the human mind comparable to the similar law relating to human society which he has in effect put forward in the first 'discourse', the basic idea here being that genius is spread evenly through-out all peoples, but that 'the chances of education and of events' either develop it or leave it buried in obscurity. The inequality in the develop-ment of knowledge which results from this is closely associated – both as cause and as effect – with that inequality in the general development of the nations concerned, which Montesquieu tries mistakenly to account for in terms of differences in climate (pp. 88–90).

In the wide-ranging accounts of the development of music, dance, poetry, history, metaphysics, physics, mathematics, logic, the arts of taste, and eloquence which follow this introduction, a number of the themes which Turgot has used before – including the 'three stages' theory – reappear yet again. The most pervasive theme, perhaps, is the simple idea that the arts and sciences come to man not from heaven but from earth – from his sensations, from his psychological and economic needs, from experiences 'which are common to and within the reach of all men' (p. 90), and that they change as these sensations, needs, and experiences change. This theme is prominent in Turgot's account of the way in which the needs of tillage and navigation developed astronomy (p. 91); the primitive origins of music, dance, and poetry (p. 91); the reason why the fables of all peoples resemble one another (p. 92); the origins of design, sculpture, and painting (p. 93); the origin of mathematics (p. 96); the 'god-making' activities of early peoples (p. 102); the reason why the English have not been able to produce any great painters (p. 103); the connection between trade and taste (p. 104); the reasons for the continua-tion of the mechanical arts when letters and taste have fallen (p. 116); the necessity for the cultivation and perfection of the mechanical arts in order that 'real physics and the higher philosophy' could arise (pp. 116–17); and in a dozen other places as well. Turgot is not consistent in his use of this theme, and it appears side by side with a number of others, but it would be absurd to pretend that it does not exist or that it is not important.

The final point I want to make about *On Universal History* is that in it Turgot goes some way towards clarifying his views about the state of perfection towards which society is advancing in the Age of Reason. In the *Philosophical Review* the general picture we get is one of an infinite advance on all fronts, of everlasting progress in every sphere, and we are apt to pass over the following significant paragraph:

Knowledge of nature and of truth is as infinite as they are: the arts, whose aim is to please us, are as limited as we are. Time constantly brings to light new discoveries in the sciences; but poetry, painting, and music have a fixed limit which the genius of languages, the imitation of nature, and the limited sensibility of our organs determine, which they attain by slow steps and which they cannot surpass. The great men of the Augustan age reached it, and are still our models.[1]

In *On Universal History* this idea is repeated (below, p. 113) and expanded a little. In particular, Turgot describes in a very interesting way the manner in which poetry, although it has already reached perfection in certain basic respects, will continue to change and progress in certain other respects as time goes on (pp. 113–14).

On Universal History finishes in midstream, just at the point where Turgot is embarking upon an interesting discussion of the way in which progress in the sciences depends upon 'inventions and technical processes'; and the great plan of a geographical-cum-sociological-cum-political treatise was never achieved. Turgot became a civil servant and statesman, and his intellectual interests turned more and more in the direction of economics.[2] Echoes of his early perfectibilist views, and, more particularly, of the theory of history with which they were associated, are however to be found scattered among some of his later works on language and literature, in some of his letters to friends,[3] and in his economic work – notably, as we shall see, in the *Reflections*. Turgot gradually became known, at any rate among a small circle,[4] as a pioneer perfectibilist, and the verbal tradition was handed on by men like Du Pont and, more importantly, Condorcet. In his *Life of Turgot*, which appeared in 1786, Condorcet described Turgot's view concerning the unbounded perfectibility of the human understanding and the limitless progress of the sciences as 'one of the great principles of his philosophy', which he 'never once abandoned'.[5] And when, a few years later, in the shadow of the guillotine, Condorcet came to write his own great work on the

---

[1] Below, p. 52.

[2] It is curious – and perhaps significant – that one of his economic works contains the first clear statement of the law of diminishing returns in agriculture, which was later to be used by Malthus and some of his contemporaries as a weapon *against* the 'perfectibilists' of their time. See below, p. 33.

[3] See, for example, his letter to Condorcet of 21 June 1772 (Schelle, III, pp. 572–4).

[4] Of whom Hume was one: see his interesting letter to Turgot of 16 June 1768 (*The Letters of David Hume*, ed. J. Y. T. Greig (Oxford, 1932), Vol. II, pp. 179–81).

[5] Condorcet, *Life of Turgot* (English translation, 1787), p. 17.

advances of the human mind, he gave Turgot his full due, placing him together with Price and Priestley as 'the first and most illustrious apostles' of the doctrine of the limitless perfectibility of the human species – that new doctrine which, in Condorcet's words, was to give 'the final blow to the already tottering structure of prejudice'.[1] Bliss was it indeed, in that dawn, to be alive.

(c) THE 'REFLECTIONS'

I have done a lot of scribbling since I saw you last [wrote Turgot to Du Pont on 9 December 1766]...I have drawn up some *Questions* for the two Chinese about whom I have spoken to you, and, in order to make their object and meaning clear, I have prefaced them with a kind of analytical sketch of the work[2] of society and of the distribution of wealth. I have not put any algebra at all in it, and there is nothing of the *Tableau Économique* but the metaphysical part; moreover, I have left on one side a large number of questions which would have to be dealt with in order to make the work complete, but I have dealt pretty thoroughly with what concerns the formation and course of capitals, interest on money, etc.; it is a kind of groundwork.[3,4]

The 'two Chinese' mentioned by Turgot, according to Du Pont, were MM. Ko and Yang, two clever young men who, after having been brought up in France by the Jesuits, were being sent back to Canton with a pension from the Crown so that they could carry on a correspondence about Chinese literature and science. Turgot gave them books, valuable instruments, the *Questions* referred to, and the *Reflections* (presumably in manuscript form).[5] But the departure of MM. Ko and Yang, who were thus unknowingly immortalised, was of course only the occasion and not the cause of the production of the *Reflections*. Even though Turgot himself described the work in a letter to Du Pont some years later as having had 'no other object than to render intelligible the questions I put to the Chinese about their country',[6] there is no need to take this too literally: Turgot was adept at finding pegs on which to hang important works, and if Ko and Yang had not conveniently presented themselves he would no doubt have found some other occasion for summarising the great system of economic theory at which he had arrived by the end of 1766.

[1] Condorcet, *Esquisse d'un Tableau Historique des Progrès de l'Esprit Humain* (Éditions Sociales, Paris, 1966), p. 221.
[2] *Travaux.*
[3] *C'est un canevas.*
[4] Schelle, II, p. 519.
[5] Du Pont, I, pp. 117–18.
[6] Schelle, III, p. 375. Cf. *ibid.* p. 676.

This system cannot be fully understood, I believe, without an appreciation of the way in which its leading propositions were connected with Turgot's historical and sociological theories. But let us leave this on one side for the time being, and consider briefly the development of Turgot's main *economic* ideas up to 1766.

Among the 'works to be written' in the extraordinary list mentioned above was a 'Treatise on circulation; interest, banking, Law's system, credit, exchange, and commerce';[1] and among Turgot's papers there is a manuscript, apparently written about 1753–4, entitled 'Plan of a Work on Commerce, the Circulation and Interest of Money, the Wealth of States', which was presumably intended as a first step in the realisation of this part of his programme.[2] This document is interesting partly because of the absence from it of any peculiarly 'Physiocratic' principles, and partly because of the presence in it of (*a*) a very clear statement of the way in which supply and demand determine the equilibrium price of a commodity,[3] which can be regarded as a first sketch of the rather more developed treatment of this subject in the *Reflections* (XXXI and XXXII);[4] (*b*) a clear statement in favour of free competition and against the regulation of prices;[5] and (*c*) a fairly clear statement, remarkable enough for its time, to the effect that free competition would establish a price for all commodities which was sufficient to cover not only the vendor's subsistence and paid-out costs, but also 'the interest on the advances which their trade[6] requires'.[7] Even if the 'vendors' referred to in the latter statement are assumed to be merchants (in the narrow sense) rather than producers, the statement when read in its context may be regarded as the germ of the *general* theory of returns to capital which was later to be used with such striking effect in the *Reflections*.

In 1759, when the celebrated Vincent de Gournay died and Marmontel asked Turgot (who had known Gournay well and been greatly influenced by him) to provide some notes about him for an obituary, Turgot wrote

[1] Schelle, I, p. 116.
[2] Schelle, I, pp. 376–87.
[3] Schelle, I, pp. 383–4. Judging from an early letter to the Abbé de Cicé, dated 7 April 1749, it would seem likely that the influence of Locke was important here (see Schelle, I, p. 146; cf. Du Pont, II, pp. 6–7).
[4] In this introduction, references in Roman numerals to the different sections of the *Reflections* follow the numbering of these sections *in the translation below*.
[5] Schelle, I, pp. 384–5. Cf. Turgot's more general plea for *'laissez-les faire...*the great, the unique principle' in the article *Fondation* which he wrote for the *Encyclopedia* three or four years later (Schelle, II, p. 591; cf. Du Pont, III, p. 250).
[6] *Commerce.*
[7] Schelle, I, p. 385.

an *Éloge*[1] which purported to summarise Gournay's economic beliefs. Whether the summary was a wholly accurate one so far as Gournay's views were concerned is rather doubtful,[2] but there is very little doubt that it represented Turgot's own views at the time. The work is note-worthy for an elaborate and uncompromising statement of the *laissez-faire* principle, and for a number of passages which indicate that Ques-nay's influence, as well as that of Gournay, was already becoming im-portant.[3] Near the beginning of the piece, Turgot ascribes to Gournay the view that 'a worker who manufactures a piece of material adds real wealth to the total wealth of the State'; and a few pages further on he similarly ascribes to him the view that 'the only real wealth which the State possesses is the annual product of its land *and of the industry of its inhabitants*', and that the sum of the revenues produced annually in the State consists of 'the net revenue of each piece of land *and the net product of the industry of each individual*'.[4] These non-Physiocratic (or perhaps deliberately anti-Physiocratic) statements, however, are followed shortly afterwards by three distinct bows in the Physiocratic direction: a favour-able reference to Quesnay's article *Corn*; a statement that it is 'agriculture and commerce, *or rather agriculture animated by commerce*' which is the source of the revenue accruing to the State; and, more important, a rather implausible ascription to Gournay of the view that 'all taxes, of whatever kind, are always in the last analysis paid by the proprietor of land'.[5] The latter statement, and the advocacy of a single tax on land rent which accompanies it, would seem at first sight to be logically incompatible with the views ascribed to Gournay earlier in the piece – and this was indeed a real problem, with which Turgot was later to wrestle in the *Reflections*. Even more important, however, is a statement in the *Éloge* to the effect that a high rate of interest 'excludes the nation from all branches of commerce of which the product is not one or two per cent above the current rate of interest'[6] – a statement which was to reappear in a general-ised and more accurate form in the *Reflections* (LXXXIX), and which sug-gests that by 1759 Turgot had already advanced a considerable way towards his general theory of the returns to capital.

[1] Schelle, I, pp. 595–623; cf. Du Pont, III, pp. 321–75.
[2] See P. Vigreux (ed.), *Turgot: Textes Choisis* (Paris, 1947), pp. 42–8, for an interesting discussion of this point.
[3] Quesnay's article *Corn*, to which Turgot makes specific reference in the *Éloge*, was published in the *Encyclopedia* in 1757.
[4] Schelle, I, pp. 600, 604, and 605 (my italics); cf. Du Pont, III, pp. 328–9, 340–1, and 341.
[5] Schelle, I, pp. 606, 608, and 609 (my italics); cf. Du Pont, III, pp. 344, 348, and 350.
[6] Schelle, I, p. 607; cf. Du Pont, III, p. 346.

Between 1759 and 1766, the date of the writing of the *Reflections*, the main intellectual influence on Turgot was of course that of Physiocracy. He would almost certainly have seen a copy of the 'third edition' of the *Tableau Économique* when Quesnay distributed it privately in 1759; and the period from 1759 to 1766 was precisely that in which almost all of the most important economic works of Quesnay and Mirabeau were published. The basic economic idea of the Physiocrats, upon which a great deal of the remainder of their system depended, was their doctrine of the exclusive 'productivity' of agriculture. It was only agriculture, they claimed, which was inherently capable of yielding a disposable surplus over necessary cost – the famous 'net product', which according to them crystallised out into land rent. Manufacture and commerce, they argued, were *not* 'productive' *in this sense* – i.e., they were not inherently capable of yielding a disposable surplus over necessary cost.[1] Turgot was evidently very impressed by this doctrine, although his own interpretation of it, and the uses to which he put it, were appreciably different from Quesnay's.

But the feature of Quesnay's work which obviously impressed Turgot more than anything else was its emphasis on the necessity of *capital* in agriculture. 'M. Quesnay', wrote Turgot in his 'Plan of a *Mémoire* on Taxes',[2] 'has dealt with the mechanism of cultivation, wholly based on very large *original advances* and demanding *annually other advances* which are equally necessary.'[3] And in the same document, Turgot gave Quesnay the credit for having been the first to lay down clearly the true distinction between *gross product* and *net product*, and 'to exclude from the *net product* the profits of the cultivator, which are the inducement, the unique and indispensable cause of cultivation'.[4] It is very significant that Turgot should have singled out the latter point, because it was precisely on this that Quesnay was *not* clear.[5] What was now required, Turgot came to believe, was (a) a generalisation of Quesnay's concept of 'advances', and its use as the basis for an explanation of the economic 'mechanism' *as a whole* – i.e., not simply for an explanation of the 'mechanism of cultivation'; and (b) a clarification and development of the idea that the profit of the entrepreneur who makes the 'advances' is part of the absolutely necessary expenses of production. Both these themes begin to appear in

[1] See my *Economics of Physiocracy* (London, 1962), pp. 379ff., and *passim*.
[2] Du Pont, IV, pp. 203–35; cf. Schelle, II, pp. 293–308. This document apparently dates from 1763.
[3] Du Pont, IV, p. 218; cf. Schelle, II, p. 302.
[4] Du Pont, IV, p. 217; cf. Schelle, II, pp. 301–2.
[5] Cf. my *Economics of Physiocracy*, pp. 297–312.

Turgot's work from about 1763 onwards.[1] By 1766 he is talking clearly about the existence and crucial importance of an entrepreneurial class – that 'precious species of men' who turn their capitals to account not only in agriculture but also 'in every other kind of commerce'.[2] What still appears to be missing is a clear recognition that 'commerce' in this connection includes not only 'commerce' in the strict sense – i.e. buying and selling – but also manufacturing. Turgot is still talking about enterprises 'in agriculture and commerce': it is not until the *Reflections* that he begins to talk clearly and consistently about 'agricultural, manufacturing, and commercial enterprises'.

In this respect, an important influence on Turgot on the eve of his composition of the *Reflections* may possibly have been that of Hume, most of whose economic essays (with which Turgot was of course quite familiar) had been published as early as 1752, and who was himself in Paris from October 1763 to January 1766. In the latter half of 1766, Turgot corresponded with Hume on the question of the incidence of taxation, and in particular on the question of the validity or otherwise of the proposition that all taxes are ultimately paid by the landowners. In one of Hume's letters to Turgot, which was apparently written in late September 1766, he made the following point:

I beg you also to consider, that, besides the Proprietors of Land and the labouring Poor, there is in every civilized Community a very large and a very opulent Body who employ their Stocks in Commerce and who enjoy a great Revenue from their giving Labour to the poorer sort. I am perswaded that in France and England the Revenue of this kind is much greater than that which arises from Land: For besides Merchants, properly speaking, I comprehend in this Class all Shop-Keepers and Master-Tradesmen of every Species. Now it is very just, that these shoud pay for the Support of the Community, which can only be where Taxes are lay'd on Consumptions. There seems to me no Pretence for saying that this order of Men are necessitated to throw their Taxes on the Proprietors of Land, since their Profits and Income can surely bear Retrenchment.[3]

Hume's explicit division of that 'very opulent Body who employ their Stocks in Commerce' into 'Merchants, properly speaking' on the one hand and 'all Shop-Keepers and Master-Tradesmen of every Species' on the other was quite remarkable for its time, and may well have helped to supply Turgot with an essential constituent of his system.

We do not know why Turgot kept the *Reflections* by him for three years

[1] Cf. Schelle, II, pp. 301, 303, 311, 314, and 402.
[2] Schelle, II, pp. 448–9; cf. Du Pont, IV, pp. 264–5.
[3] *The Letters of David Hume*, ed. J. Y. T. Greig (Oxford, 1932), II, p. 94.

before sending it to Du Pont for publication, or whether the work was changed and developed in any way during those three years. So far as the first question is concerned, it is possible that Turgot was waiting to see how *Éphémérides* would progress under Du Pont's editorship; but it seems rather more likely that he was hoping that he might find time to 'make something passable'[1] of a piece which, however much thought may have gone into the making of its basic propositions, was no doubt written down hastily and with perhaps a little more than passing reference to the occasion of the departure of MM. Ko and Yang. On the second question, it would seem unlikely that any really substantial changes were made in the work during the period concerned. The significant thing here is that during those three years Turgot's ideas on a number of the subjects treated in the *Reflections* underwent a certain amount of development. In his notes on the *mémoires* which Graslin and Saint-Péravy submitted in 1767 for a prize offered by the Royal Agricultural Society of Limoges, for example, Turgot not only put forward his famous statement of the law of diminishing returns, but also appreciably clarified his analysis of the nature of entrepreneurial profit[2] – an analysis carried to a still higher stage in his letters of October–December 1770 to Terray on the corn trade.[3] Yet there is no real trace of any of these developments in the *Reflections*.

Turning now to the *Reflections* itself, one of the most interesting things about it is the way in which the staggeringly 'modern' theory of capital in which it culminates, and the basic 'Physiocratic' theory of production of which it makes use, are both set within the context of a broad historical and sociological analysis, deriving from Turgot's early works of the Sorbonne period. Turgot's intellectual development in this respect mirrored that of his great contemporary Adam Smith and anticipated that of Marx: all three began with some kind of 'materialist' theory of history, and then went on to develop from this a system of economics which in one way or another embodied or made use of its basic propositions. It is perfectly possible, of course, if one wishes, to abstract Turgot's theory of capital from its context and present it purely as an anticipation

---

[1] See below, p. 37. It is worthy of note that the manuscript which Turgot sent to Du Pont on 2 December 1769 was in working copy form (Schelle, III, p. 74). The statement by Du Pont, in his foreword to the *Reflections* in *Éphémérides*, to the effect that he had for a very long time been begging Turgot to let him have the work, is hardly consistent with Turgot's statement, in his letter to Du Pont of 1 December 1766 (Schelle, III, p. 72) that he would be sending him 'a' (not '*the*') 'piece on wealth'.

[2] Schelle, II, pp. 626–58; cf. Du Pont, IV, pp. 312–64.

[3] Schelle, III, pp. 265–354; cf. Du Pont, VI, pp. 120–291.

of the best nineteenth-century analytical work in this field – which it indeed was.[1] But by doing this alone, one tends to underestimate the brilliance of Turgot's achievement, and cuts oneself off from any hope of understanding the way in which the 'modern' and 'Physiocratic' parts of his analysis were related to one another.

Turgot's main aim in the *Reflections* was to investigate the way in which the economic 'machine' operated in a society where there were three main classes or 'orders' of economic agents – landowners, wage-earners, *and capitalist entrepreneurs*. His very postulation of an entrepreneurial society of this kind was a highly remarkable achievement, given the time and place in which he was working: Turgot evidently possessed to the full that peculiar feature of genius which sometimes allows it not only to observe what *is* typical, but also to discern and analyse what is *becoming* typical. But even more remarkable was the way in which he appreciated, whether consciously or unconsciously, that one could arrive at an understanding in depth of such a society by beginning with an analysis of the working of the 'machine' *in the type of society which historically preceded it*, and then asking oneself what alterations in its working were brought about when a new class of capitalist entrepreneurs entered upon the historic scene. This is a methodological device which was later to be used very effectively by Smith, Ricardo, and Marx;[2] the only real difference between their approach and Turgot's – and it is indeed a significant difference – is that whereas the preceding state of society which they postulated was one in which there were neither landlords nor capitalists, so that the labourer owned what Smith called 'the whole produce of his labour',[3] that which Turgot postulated was one in which landlords – although not of course capitalists – *did* exist.

What Turgot did, in effect, was to accept the view – already adumbrated by Quesnay and Mirabeau in their *Philosophie Rurale*[4] and later to be developed by the Scottish Historical School – that after the hunting, pastoral, and agricultural stages society proceeded to a fourth stage – the so-called 'commercial' stage; to assume that in this fourth stage a capitalist or entrepreneurial form of organisation was paramount; and to analyse this form of society by examining the way in which it arose from and impinged upon the 'agricultural' stage and altered the basic relations which were characteristic of it.

---

[1] Cf. J. A. Schumpeter, *History of Economic Analysis* (London, 1954), pp. 243–9.
[2] See my *Economics and Ideology* (London, 1967), pp. 96–8.
[3] Adam Smith, *Wealth of Nations*, Book I, chapter VI.
[4] See my *Economics of Physiocracy*, p. 62.

Turgot's starting-point in the *Reflections*, then, is a society which has already proceeded through the hunting and pastoral stages (LIV) to the *agricultural stage*. This society is characterised (*a*) by the social division of labour and the mutual exchange of the products of the different kinds of labour (I–IV); (*b*) by a basic social division between the class of cultivators, which is 'productive' in the sense that the fertility of the soil enables it to produce a surplus over subsistence, and the class of artisans, which is 'stipendiary' in the sense that it is in effect supported by this surplus (V–VIII);[1] (*c*) by the eventual emergence of a 'disposable' class of private landowners, to whom the surplus or 'net product' of the land accrues in the form of 'revenue' (IX–XVIII); and (*d*) by the existence of various different arrangements which the landowners may make with the cultivators in order to get their land cultivated and to ensure that they receive the 'net product' (XIX–XXVIII). These arrangements, which are dealt with in more or less the order in which they actually appeared on the historic scene, culminate in 'tenant-farming, or the letting-out of Land' (XXVI). The importance of the latter kind of arrangement, as the sequel shows, is that the farmers to whom the land is leased are *capitalist entrepreneurs*, who make all the 'advances' involved in cultivation and pay the landowners the 'net product' in the form of an annual rent.

Having at last – one quarter of the way through the book – introduced the concept of *capital*,[2] Turgot proceeds immediately (XXIX) to the subject of 'capitals in general, and of the revenue of money', thereby making the vital transition from the agricultural society which was his historical (and analytical) starting-point to the specifically *capitalist* or *entrepreneurial* society which it was his main concern to examine. He begins with what may appear at first sight to be a digression (XXX–XLVIII) on the use of gold and silver in commerce and the general principles according to which the prices of exchangeable commodities are determined in a competitive market. A 'digression' of this kind, however, over-long though it may perhaps be, was essential in order to set the stage for much of what was to

---

[1] These sections, if read in abstraction, might at first sight appear to embody 'Physiocratic' preconceptions of the most dogmatic and indefensible kind. It should be remembered, however, (*a*) that Turgot is at this stage deliberately abstracting from the distinction between 'the Husbandman and the Proprietor of the land' (IX); and (*b*) that he is really doing no more than translate into formal economic terms the familiar proposition, which he himself had put forward early in his *Philosophical Review*, that 'tillage...is able to feed more men than are employed in it...Hence towns, trade, the useful arts and accomplishments, the division of occupations', etc. (see below, p. 43).

[2] There is a passing reference to 'advances' in XVI, but this is clearly inconsistent with the context. It looks very like an insertion by Du Pont.

follow. *Capitals* are then reintroduced, and the historical process of their accumulation – at first in the form of various items of 'movable wealth' and then in the form of money – is briefly discussed (XLIX–L).

The ordering of the sections which immediately follow leaves something to be desired: it is not always easy, as Turgot found at this point, to make history and analysis run hand in hand. But the main lines of his argument are clear enough. 'Advances' in the form of movable wealth are necessary in every occupation (LI). They are necessary, first, in *agriculture*, where they have historically taken various different forms (LII–LV), and where the demands of large-scale cultivation (LXIV) lead to the separation of the broad class of cultivators into ordinary wage-earners and 'Entrepreneurs or Capitalists who make all the advances' (LXV), the latter necessarily receiving, over and above the return of their capital, their 'wages', and compensation for their various costs, 'a profit equal to the revenue they could acquire with their capital without any labour' (LXII–LXIII). They are necessary, second, in *manufacture and industry* (LIX), where large-scale production leads similarly to the separation of the industrial stipendiary class into 'ordinary Workmen' and 'capitalist Entrepreneurs' (LX–LXI), each of the latter necessarily receiving, over and above the return of his capital, his 'wages', and compensation for his various costs, 'a profit sufficient to compensate him for what his money would have been worth to him if he had employed it in the acquisition of an estate' (LX). And they are necessary, finally, in *commerce*, in respect of which a similar analysis leads to similar conclusions (LXVI–LXVII). This picture of a society in which, behind the veil of money, we see the whole of agriculture, industry, and commerce depending upon the continual advance and return of capitals owned by a great entrepreneurial class (LXVIII–LXX), was extraordinarily advanced for its time.

In a society of this kind, Turgot explains, capital may be invested not only in agricultural, industrial, and commercial enterprises, but also in the purchase of *land*, the revenue from which will then in effect constitute the return on the capital so invested (LVI–LVIII, LXXXIII, and LXXXV). Or, alternatively, the capital may simply be lent out to a borrower in return for interest on it at an agreed rate (LXXI). This loan transaction, in essence, is one in which the *use of money* is bought and sold; and the price of this use of money is determined, like the prices of all other commodities, 'by the haggling which takes place between the seller and buyer, by the balance of supply and demand' (LXXI–LXXII), and not, as a number of earlier economists had believed, by the quantity of money (LXXVII–LXXIX). The receipt of interest is morally justifiable, in spite of the contrary view expressed by certain theologians (LXXIII–LXXV); and the level of the rate of interest ought never to be fixed by law (LXXVI). Turgot's theory of interest, with its clear recognition that 'the rate of interest is relative to the quantity of values accumulated and put into reserve in order to create capitals' (LXXX–LXXXII), represents a considerable advance over Hume's theory; and there is some substance in Schumpeter's claim that it was 'not only by far the greatest performance in the field of interest theory the eighteenth century produced but it clearly foreshadowed much of the best thought of the last decades of the nineteenth.'[1]

After a 'recapitulation of the five different methods of employing capitals' (LXXXIII), Turgot goes on to explain the way in which the returns to capital in these different employments are, as he puts it, 'mutually limited by one another' (LXXXIV). The basic idea lying behind the four sections which follow would seem to be that if there were no differences in the trouble and risk involved in the different uses of capital, an equilibrium situation would be reached in which the rates of return on capital were equal in all these uses. Since there are in fact marked differences in the trouble and risk involved, however, the equilibrium situation actually reached is characterised not by an equality but by an inequality of returns – capital invested in land bringing in the least (LXXXV), capital lent out at interest bringing in a little more (LXXXVI), and capital invested in agricultural, manufacturing, and commercial enterprises bringing in the most (LXXXVII), so that equilibrium is perfectly compatible with inequality of returns and indeed necessarily produces it (LXXXVIII). It follows, according to Turgot, that the rate of interest is the 'thermometer'[2] of the extent to which production will be carried: if interest were at five per cent, for example, no agricultural, manufacturing, or commercial enterprises which were incapable of yielding a net return higher than this would in fact be undertaken (LXXXIX–XC) – once again a very 'modern' proposition.

After two sections dealing with certain problems of social accounting (XCI–XCII), Turgot proceeds to his final task – to ask what essential difference, if any, was made to the basic relations characteristic of the simple 'agricultural' society with which he had started by the impingement upon it of the new class of capitalist entrepreneurs. The coming of the new class had certainly resulted in the division of the productive class and the stipendiary class into capitalists and labourers: but did this

---

[1] Schumpeter, *History of Economic Analysis*, p. 332.
[2] Cf. Hume's statement, in his essay *Of Interest*, that 'interest is the barometer of the state' (*David Hume: Writings on Economics*, ed. E. Rotwein (London, 1955), p. 55).

necessarily mean that the basic relations previously existing between the productive class as a whole and the stipendiary class as a whole, and between these two classes and the disposable class, now no longer existed? The way in which Turgot himself formulated the question was simply this: 'Let us now see how what we have just said about the different methods of employing capitals squares with what we previously laid down about the division of all the members of Society into three classes – the productive class, or that of agriculturists, the industrial or commercial class, and the disposable class, or that of proprietors' (XCIII).

In the agricultural society, it will be remembered, the product of the labour of the (undifferentiated) productive class had been sufficient not only to provide its own wages, but also to provide a *net* product, or revenue, which accrued in one form or another to the proprietors of the land. This revenue alone was 'disposable' (XIV), in the sense that it did not have to be earmarked for use in the reproduction of the annual product at the same level in the following year;[1] and the class of proprietors which received it was itself also 'disposable', in the sense that its members were not 'earmarked' for any particular kind of work (XV). And it was the expenditure of this revenue by the proprietors, together with the expenditure of the cultivators, which was conceived to generate the incomes of the third social class (XVII), which for this reason was called the stipendiary class (XV).

How, then, is this picture altered when capitals and capitalist entrepreneurs are introduced? At first sight the alterations would seem to be very radical indeed. For, in the first place, if agriculture, manufacture, and commerce are to be maintained, the entrepreneurs in these occupations must now receive a return which is sufficient not only to secure for them their subsistence, the refund of their capital, and compensation for their paid-out costs, but also to provide a net 'profit' sufficiently high to prevent them from transferring their capital out of the particular sector concerned and either investing it in the purchase of land or lending it out at interest. Turgot's discussions of this 'profit' are somewhat vague: there are hardly two places in which he describes it in exactly the same way, and one is never really clear what precisely it is supposed to be a reward *for*, or indeed whether it can be said to be a 'reward' at all.[2] But whatever

---

[1] Turgot's clearest definition of 'disposable' in this connection is to be found not in the *Reflections* but in his fifth letter to Terray (14 November 1770), where he says that 'it is only this net product which is *disposable*; it is only this portion of the fruits of the earth which is indispensably earmarked (*affectée*) for the reproduction of the following year' (Schelle, III, p. 292; cf. Du Pont, VI, p. 170).

[2] His clearest and most useful description is probably that in the fifth letter to Terray

it actually is, and wherever it actually comes from, there is no doubt that its level will be sufficiently high to enable its recipients to live at well above the subsistence level; and the question therefore arises as to whether this part of the entrepreneur's income is in fact 'disposable', so that in the entrepreneurial society the rent of land is no longer the *only* 'disposable' (and taxable) form of income (XCV). And, in the second place, the interest on money placed on loan, and the recipient of this interest, would both also appear at first sight to be 'disposable', thereby raising a rather similar problem (XCIV–XCVIII).

The problem of the entrepreneurs' 'profit', Turgot believed, was fairly easy to deal with. If we define a 'disposable' income as one whose receipt is not absolutely necessary in order to ensure that an enterprise carries on its operations next year at the same level (at least) as it is carrying them on this year,[1] then the 'profit' of the entrepreneur is definitely *not* 'disposable', since if it is not received the enterprise will not be carried on at all. What Turgot was doing here, in effect, was to argue that in an entrepreneurial society the 'absolutely necessary' receipts must be taken to include not only compensation for paid-out and subsistence costs (which was all that they normally included in a simple agricultural society), but also a risk and 'special ability' premium, and compensation for the *opportunity cost* involved in employing one's capital in the enterprise concerned rather than investing it in the purchase of land or lending it out at interest.

The problem of interest was more difficult, because the recipient of interest, unlike the entrepreneur, is indeed clearly 'disposable' so far as his person is concerned (XCIV); and at first sight it would appear that the interest itself is also 'disposable', since 'the entrepreneur and the enterprise can do without it' (XCV). The way in which Turgot gets over this is simple enough, in essence, although his argument becomes rather tortuous at this point. What he does, in effect, is to put a further gloss on the concept of 'absolutely necessary' receipts. If the operations of enterprises over the economy as a whole are to be maintained at their existing level, then it is not only 'absolutely necessary' that each entrepreneur should receive a sufficient amount of 'profit' to prevent him from closing down his enterprise and becoming a landowner or money-lender, but it is

(Schelle, III, p. 292; cf. Du Pont, VI, pp. 170-1). Some commentators have seized on Turgot's use of the verb *attendre* at one point in LX to ascribe a 'waiting' theory to him, but this seems to me to be unduly selective: one might just as easily father an 'exploitation' theory upon him on the basis of the wording in LXI.
[1] Cf. above, p. 24.

also 'absolutely necessary' that the class of money-lenders should receive a rate of interest which is not artificially reduced below its market level (e.g. by taxing it). For, says Turgot, if this interest is 'encroached upon', the rate charged on advances to all enterprises will increase, thereby causing the operations of the enterprises themselves to be reduced (XCVI). Thus the interest received by money-lending capitalists is very different from the revenue received by landowners (XCVII–XCVIII), and the latter is revealed as being still the only *truly* 'disposable' (and therefore taxable) form of income in the entrepreneurial society (XCIX). It also still remains true that the wages and profits of the industrial and commercial classes are 'paid either by the proprietor out of his revenue, or by the agents of the productive class out of the part which is earmarked for their needs' (XCIX), so that the adjective 'stipendiary' still correctly describes them; and there is even a sense – although a somewhat rarefied one – in which capitals themselves 'come from the land' (C).[1]

How far does all this make Turgot a Physiocrat? He certainly used a great deal of the Physiocrats' economic terminology – although he clearly objected to the use of the unnecessarily inflammatory adjective 'sterile' to describe the industrial and commercial classes.[2] He accepted Quesnay's crucial concept of 'advances' – although he generalised and developed it out of all recognition. He accepted the Physiocrats' basic class stratification – although not really as much more than a kind of historical and logical starting-point. He accepted, in a sense, the quite basic Physiocratic doctrine that land rent was the only 'disposable' (and taxable) income – although the arguments which enabled him to reach this conclusion for an entrepreneurial (as distinct from an agricultural) society owed relatively little to Physiocratic inspiration, and were in some respects anti-Physiocratic. Finally, he accepted the Physiocratic idea that the incomes of the industrial and commercial classes were 'paid' by agriculture – although he put a distinctive gloss of his own on this idea too. To describe him as a Physiocrat, then, would be as wrong as to describe him as a non-Physiocrat, or for that matter as anything else. 'I may be wrong,' wrote Turgot to Du Pont in 1770, 'but everyone wants to be himself, and not another...All your additions tend to make me out to be an economist,[3]

---

[1] Section CI, tacked on at the end, is of importance primarily because of its assertion (made more or less in passing) that savings are converted *immediately* into investment. See below, p. 31).

[2] The word 'sterile' is used only once in the *Reflections* – in XVIII, where it presumably appears in order to provide a kind of cross-reference to Physiocratic writings.

[3] 'Economist' was used at this time not in its modern sense, but as the equivalent of 'Physiocrat'.

something which I do not want to be any more than an encyclopedist.'[1]
So although he himself was prepared to say that he was a disciple of
Quesnay *and Gournay*,[2] he would probably have preferred not to be
regarded as anyone's disciple. 'Would you care to join my following?'
asked the Comte de Guiche. 'No sir', answered Cyrano de Bergerac, 'I do
not follow.'

(d) SOCIOLOGY, ECONOMICS, AND PROGRESS

Turgot's *On Universal History*, as we have seen, stopped short at the
point where he had begun enlarging upon the role of the 'mechanical
arts' in the development of society, and the great work on geography,
sociology, and politics which he had projected was never in fact achieved.
What emerged instead was the theory of an entrepreneurial economy
which he sketched out in the *Reflections*. In this respect, as I have already
said, Turgot's intellectual development was very similar to that of Smith
and Marx: all three thinkers began by working out the elements of a
universal 'sociological' system, embodying a theory of history which laid
emphasis on economic causes, and then developed *from* these 'sociological'
systems the great systems of economic theory by which we mainly know
them today.

The basic concept which united the 'sociological' and 'economic'
systems, in the case of all three thinkers, was the revolutionary idea that
the historical processes of social development, and the manner in which
any particular society (or economy) operated, were not arbitrary, but
were in an important sense 'subject to law'. What had happened in history, and what was happening in contemporary society, reflected the
working of certain law-governed, almost mechanistic processes, which
operated independently of the wills of individual men, and which it was
the task of the social scientist to analyse and explain. In Turgot's sociology, we see the beginnings of this idea in, for example, his account of
the way in which the evil passions of ambitious princes promoted progress; in his theory that the mathematical frequency of the appearance of
geniuses was constant; and in a number of his biological and mechanical
analogies. In his economics, we see the idea again in a rather different
form: the concept of the economy as a kind of great 'machine', always
tending of itself to bring about a situation of 'equilibrium', becomes quite
central. It emerges very clearly, for example, in a letter which Turgot

---

[1] Schelle, III, p. 374.
[2] Schelle, I, p. 507.

wrote to Hume on 25 March 1767, where he speaks of 'a kind of equilibrium' which establishes itself between certain economic quantities; of the way in which, if one of the 'weights' is changed, 'it is impossible that there should not result from this in the whole of the machine a movement which tends to re-establish the old equilibrium'; and of the way in which 'in every complicated machine, there are frictions which delay the results most infallibly demonstrated by theory'.[1]

It remained true, of course, that society and its history were made by human beings; but the important point was that they were not, in general, made consciously, but emerged as what I have called above[2] a kind of unintended by-product of the conflict of human wills and actions which were often directed towards quite different ends. There is already an inkling of this in a passage in *L'Esprit des Lois*, where Montesquieu, talking about the principle of monarchy, says:

It is with this kind of government as with the system of the universe, in which there is a power that constantly repels all bodies from the centre, and a power of gravitation that attracts them to it. Honor sets all the parts of the body politic in motion, and by its very action connects them; thus each individual advances the public good, while he only thinks of promoting his own interest.[3]

And there is much more than an inkling of it, as we have seen,[4] in Turgot's analogy of the army 'directed by some mighty genius'.

The fact that men in their social and economic life were 'subject to law' did not of course mean, in Turgot's view, that free will was an illusion. Nor did it mean that the heavens were empty. Providence still existed, and still in a sense worked through men, but it did so in a much more remote and roundabout way than most of the ecclesiastical practitioners of 'universal history' had thought. Bossuet, for example, in his celebrated *Discourse on Universal History*, had argued that God controlled human affairs in part directly, by influencing great men on strategic occasions, and in part indirectly, by bringing it about that all the parts of the whole depended upon one another, and by 'preparing the effects in the most distant causes'.[5] Even though this account left the 'particular causes' of historical events as a worth-while subject of study, Turgot felt that it still gave far too much weight to the influence of Providence. The

---

[1] Schelle, II, pp. 658–65. This letter also contains some interesting comments on Rousseau's ideas about the successive advances of the human mind.
[2] P. 11.
[3] *The Spirit of the Laws* (Hafner Library of Classics, New York, 1949), p. 25.
[4] Above, p. 11.
[5] Bossuet, *Discours sur L'Histoire Universelle*, ed. M. Lefèvre (Paris, 1859), Part III, chapters 1, 2, and 8, *passim*.

most that it could be assumed that the latter had done was to create a law-governed universe in which the complex interplay of cause and effect was likely to produce a long-run – but often very slow and unsteady – tendency towards perfection. It was only in this rather attenuated sense, then, that the world could be said to be 'the most glorious witness to the wisdom which presides over it'.[1] And the purpose of social science was simply to analyse the processes whereby history, as it were, made itself and the economy ran itself. If the results of this analysis turned out to justify the ways of God to man, then that was all to the good, but it was not the primary object of the exercise.

Up to a point, then, it is true to say that Turgot's theory of history was put forward as an alternative to the 'Providential' theories of men like Bossuet. And it is also no doubt true that Turgot, like all of us on such occasions, was influenced more than he knew by the very doctrines which he was combating. The parallels between Turgot's and Bossuet's work are certainly quite striking. Bossuet had talked in terms of a succession of religious 'epochs'; Turgot talked in terms of a succession of socio-economic 'stages'. Bossuet had emphasised the way in which God worked through individual law-givers and conquerors, so that although they made history they did not make it as they wished; Turgot emphasised the way in which certain historical laws and necessities worked through them, with much the same kind of result. Bossuet had proclaimed that 'all the great empires which we have seen on earth have led in different ways towards the good of religion and the glory of God';[2] Turgot proclaimed that through all its vicissitudes mankind in the long run advances towards greater perfection.

But there is no need to go all the way with Professor Baillie, who has described the eighteenth-century doctrine of progress as 'essentially a redisposition of the Christian ideas which it seeks to replace'.[3] There is no doubt that Turgot's version of the doctrine of progress was influenced in an important way by these 'Christian ideas', but there were other important influences as well. One, obviously, was the spectacular progress of the sciences in the seventeenth and eighteenth centuries, which led many others besides Turgot to conclude that no bounds could be put to their further development. Another, perhaps equally important, was the stimulus afforded by the succession of studies of the Indian tribes of

---

[1] Below, p. 71.

[2] Bossuet, *Discours sur L'Histoire Universelle*, p. 432.

[3] J. Baillie, *The Belief in Progress* (Oxford, 1950), p. 113. Cf. C. L. Becker, *The Heavenly City of the Eighteenth-Century Philosophers* (New Haven, 1932), *passim*.

North America which had appeared earlier in the century. If, as everyone
soon came to appreciate, 'our ancestors and the Pelasgians who preceded
the Greeks were like the savages of America',[1] then it was fairly obvious
that something which most people would want to call 'progress' had been
taking place since the time of the Pelasgians.[2]

If we want to regard Turgot as the unconscious vehicle of some kind of
zeitgeist, surely we would be on safer ground looking in his work for
'bourgeois' rather than for 'Christian' currents. Professor Pollard has
gone so far as to say that Turgot 'personifies the French bourgeoisie in
the full flower of its hope';[3] and it is certainly true that if we look at his
life's work as a whole – not only his sociology and his economic theory,
but also his practical work as an administrator – it appears more of a piece
when looked at from this viewpoint than from any other. Even if one is
not prepared to see anything distinctively 'bourgeois' in his respect for
English rights and liberties, his worship of science, his faith in reason, and
his immense optimism about the future of mankind, one can surely not
deny the aptness of the label when applied, say, to his numerous statements to the effect that 'the State has the greatest interest in conserving
the mass of capitals',[4] and above all, to the theoretical system of the
Reflections.

There is no doubt that the system of the *Reflections* is basically 'capitalist', and that the particular form of 'capitalism' which it envisages and
analyses is by no means a primitive one. This can be brought home if one
contrasts Turgot's system with Cantillon's, which was certainly the most
advanced prior to Turgot's and from which Turgot may well have learned
a great deal. Chapter XIII of Part One of Cantillon's *Essay on the Nature
of Commerce in General*, indeed, reads at first sight rather like a concise
summary of the *Reflections*. The very heading of the chapter – 'The
circulation and exchange of produce and commodities, as well as their
production, are carried on in Europe by Entrepreneurs, and at a risk'[5] –
is reminiscent enough; and the content of the chapter, with its distinction
between entrepreneurs and hired people,[6] its emphasis on the way in
which all entrepreneurs bear risks, and its association (in certain cases) of

[1] Below, p. 89.
[2] Another point, which cannot be elaborated here, is that contemporary controversies
about the origin of the Indians may have contributed in an important way to the
emergence of the 'three stages' theory of development.
[3] S. Pollard, *The Idea of Progress* (London, 1968), p. 78.
[4] Schelle, II, p. 301. Cf. *ibid*. II, pp. 314 and 448–9, and V, p 244.
[5] Cantillon, *Essai sur la Nature du Commerce en Générale*, ed. H. Higgs (London, 1931),
p. 46.
[6] *Gens à gages*.

entrepreneurship with capital,[1] is even more so. When one looks into it, however, the differences between Cantillon's and Turgot's accounts are seen to be rather more striking than the resemblances. With Cantillon, the 'entrepreneurs' include those who are 'Entrepreneurs of their own labour without any capital' – chimney sweeps, water carriers, and even beggars and robbers; with Turgot, all entrepreneurs are assumed to be employers of labour, and independent workmen and artisans do not enter the picture at all. With Cantillon, although the fact that an entrepreneur may set himself up with a capital to conduct his enterprise is quite often mentioned, it is not particularly emphasised; with Turgot, the large capitals or 'advances' assumed to be employed by entrepreneurs are constantly emphasised and play a crucial role in the working of the system as a whole. With Cantillon, finally, the 'profit' of the entrepreneur seems to be regarded as a kind of superior but unfixed wage; with Turgot, there is a much sharper differentiation between the profit of the entrepreneur and the wage of the hired workman. Clearly Cantillon is analysing a society where the capitalist entrepreneur is just beginning to separate himself out from the ranks of the independent workmen; Turgot on the other hand is analysing a society where it is assumed that this process has been completed and that the capitalist system has consolidated itself in all fields of economic activity.

Now the interesting and important thing about all this is that in contemporary France, and even in contemporary England, a capitalist system of this kind was very far from having in fact emerged: at most, it was in the process of emerging. And Turgot, of course, was well aware of this: having spent thirteen years of his life working in the backward but not untypical provinces of Limousin and Angoumois he could hardly have been under any illusions about it. In Turgot's France, capitalism had some hold in agriculture, but only in certain areas; it had very little hold in 'manufacture', which was quite largely carried on by independent workmen; and competition was seriously restricted in almost every field of activity. Yet in the *Reflections* we have a clear picture of an economy in which capitalism embraces all spheres of production; in which the 'industrious' classes are divided sharply into entrepreneurs and wage-earners; in which free competition is universal and there appears to be no monopoly whatsoever; in which even landownership seems to be little more than just another form of investment of capital; and in which there is no possibility of a 'general glut of commodities' because savings are transformed immediately into investment.

[1] Usually *fond* or *fonds*, rarely *capital*.

This marked gap between the model and contemporary reality would not have appeared in any way mysterious to Turgot's readers, assuming that the latter were by this time familiar with the writings of the Physiocrats. Quesnay, in order to draw attention in a striking way to the backwardness of the contemporary economy, had adopted the device of beginning with an analytical model of the economy in what he called 'a state of prosperity'. This model was in part descriptive, in the sense that it contained certain elements which were already evident on the surface of contemporary reality; in part predictive, in the sense that it embodied the assumption that certain current trends had continued and intensified; and in part a kind of ideal, in the sense that it was assumed to represent a highly desirable state of affairs towards the attainment of which government policies should properly be directed.[1] Turgot's model of an entrepreneurial society in the *Reflections* was of precisely the same general type,[2] and would have been clearly recognised as such by the majority of his readers, at any rate in France. They would also have recognised the essential difference between Quesnay's model and Turgot's – that in the former capitalism was assumed to be paramount only in agriculture, whereas in the latter it was assumed to be paramount in every field of economic activity. And they would not have been misled by the absence in the *Reflections* of any elaborate panegyrics in praise of the postulated system into believing that the model was intended to be merely descriptive and predictive, and not in addition an ideal to which Turgot felt it was quite practicable and eminently desirable that society should endeavour to attain. As such, they would almost certainly have regarded it as part and parcel of Turgot's general doctrine of progress.

But before we ourselves accept it as such, and as yet another reflection of the views of 'the French bourgeoisie in the full flower of its hope', there are two qualifications which must be made. In the first place, we do not get any clear picture in the *Reflections* of an economy which is capable of continuous and indefinite advance: rather, we get a picture of an economy which, in some respects at any rate, has reached a kind of ceiling – even if a very high one – and which is subject to certain important constraints on

---

[1] Cf. my *Economics of Physiocracy*, pp. 273–4 and 377–9.

[2] 'Let us suppose, then, the state of full prosperity, with production and commerce animated by a general competition, by the circulation of capitals proportionate to the total of the agricultural and commercial enterprises of which the Kingdom is capable, the return of the revenue to reproduction through expenditure following, without any obstacles, its natural course.' This supposition, made by Turgot about 1763 in a note on the effects of indirect taxes (Schelle, II, p. 311), is very similar to that made in the *Reflections*.

further development. For example, 'the wage of the Workman is limited to what is necessary in order to enable him to procure his subsistence' (VI), and there is no suggestion that he can ever expect any more than this.[1] There appears to be no guarantee that the rate of interest fixed by the market will be low enough to enable a nation to carry its industry and agriculture to the full extent of its potential (LXXXIX–XC). There is no built-in specification about technological progress, and the main emphasis in the model is more on its static than on its dynamic aspects. And if we incorporate into the model, as we probably should, the law of diminishing returns in agriculture which Turgot formulated in 1767,[2] it becomes even more evident that his optimism and hope were tempered by a fairly healthy sense of realism.

In the second place, although Turgot's 'capitalism' was relatively advanced as compared with Cantillon's, it was still relatively backward as compared with Adam Smith's. Smith's capitalists, generally speaking, are not themselves 'industrious': they use their capital to employ labour, and receive, over and above the return of their paid-out costs and interest on their capital at the normal rate, a *net* income, profit, which is as it were exuded by the capital–labour relationship, and which bears a regular proportion not to the effort, if any, which they expend but to the value of the capital they have invested. Turgot's capitalists, on the other hand, are definitely 'industrious', and the 'profit' which they receive from their enterprises is not clearly differentiated from the wages of their labour or the interest on their capital. Nor is this 'profit' exuded by the capital–labour relationship: basically, it is simply a risk and 'special ability' premium plus compensation for an opportunity cost whose level is determined by the general demand-and-supply situation.[3] Smith's capitalists, again, are an independent class, standing on their own, whose income is as it were original rather than derived. Turgot's industrial and commercial capitalists, on the other hand, are still a 'stipendiary' class, and their incomes are 'paid either by the proprietor out of his revenue, or by the agents of the productive class'...[4] Clearly Turgot was unable completely to transcend the limitations of the 'agricultural' framework within which the analysis in the first part of the *Reflections* was set. The flower of the French bourgeoisie's hope was still rooted – even if only loosely – in feudal soil.

[1] The only gleam of hope is in section L.
[2] Schelle, II, pp. 643–6; cf. Du Pont, IV, pp. 314–20.
[3] See above, p. 25.
[4] See above, p. 26.

Appendices to the Introduction

In the interests of readability I have appended no 'translator's notes' at all to the English texts which follow. In their place I offer the following comments on the general principles I have adopted in translating them, and on particular difficulties which arose in the case of each.

a. General

Although Turgot's distinctive style is recognisable enough in each of the three pieces, it varies considerably from one to the other owing to the different purposes which they were intended to fulfil. The first is, in form at least, a piece of oratory; the second is an elaborate set of notes for a larger work, probably not revised by the author and certainly not completed; and the third is a closely argued and relatively polished piece of economic analysis in a highly compressed form. In translating the three texts, I have not attempted to disguise the oratorical flights of the first, the rather haphazard and unbalanced nature of parts of the second, and the somewhat staccato character of much of the third. Nor have I attempted to clean up the more obscure and long-winded passages: the only real concession I have made here is to simplify the punctuation in certain places, while leaving intact enough of the ubiquitous colons and semi-colons to preserve something of the true flavour of the original. Turgot is usually such a refreshingly clear and concrete thinker that occasional archaisms and awkwardnesses of style do not really hinder intelligibility: my translation therefore tends to be literal rather than imaginative.

b. The 'Philosophical Review'

In the light of Turgot's main theme in this piece, it seemed justifiable to translate *perfectionner*, in almost all places, as 'to perfect' rather than 'to improve'. Similarly *progrès* is normally translated as 'progress', except where (as in the title of the piece) the plural form of the word renders 'advances' necessary as a substitute.

Mélange, *mêler*, etc., I have usually translated (sometimes at the cost of a little awkwardness) as 'intermingling', 'to intermingle', etc. *Fixé* is sometimes 'fixed', but more often 'stabilised' and occasionally 'immobilised'. *Mœurs*, always a difficult word to translate, is sometimes 'manners', sometimes 'customs', and on one occasion 'behaviour'. I have simply done the best I could with *la police* and *la politique*, which are inevitably stumbling-blocks.

A special note is required about the important passage on p. 42 which I have for better or worse translated as 'The most exalted mental attainments are only and can only be a development or combination of the original ideas based on sensation'. The French text reads '*Les connaissances les plus sublimes ne sont et ne peuvent être que les premières idées sensibles développées ou combinées*'. Later in the piece (p. 46), I have translated the adjective *sensible* simply as 'sensible', meaning here 'perceptible by the senses'.

c. 'On Universal History'

Since *On Universal History* is essentially a development of some of the leading ideas in the *Philosophical Review*, and since a number of passages and phrases from the first are reproduced more or less exactly in the second, I have tried to translate these similarly in both places, so that when divergences occur in the translation the reader can be reasonably certain that they occur also in the original.

The comments I have made in (*b*) above on the translation of specific words apply *mutatis mutandis* to *On Universal History* as well. The difficulties surrounding the translation of *sensible* and associated words become greater, of course, in the second 'discourse', where Turgot deals much more extensively with metaphysics. Generally speaking the argument of the second 'discourse' is more difficult to follow than that of the first, partly because Turgot is there dealing with more difficult subjects and partly because his treatment of them sometimes tends to be a little obscure. My only principle of translation here has been to ensure that the English is at any rate no more difficult to follow than the original French. It may help in the comprehension of the second 'discourse' to know that the word 'analogy' is usually employed in its etymological sense.

d. The 'Reflections'

An exceptionally large number of difficulties arises in the *Reflections* because of the dual meanings of certain words which are frequently used in the text. *Argent* in most contexts is translated as 'money', but in places where it clearly refers to the monetary metal it is usually translated as 'silver'. *Bestiaux* is usually 'live-stock', but in one or two places the context requires 'cattle'. *Commerce* is usually 'commerce', but in some places where this would appear unduly archaic 'trade' is used. *Culture* in certain contexts is 'cultivation', but in others it has to be 'agriculture'. *Denier* can mean 'rate of interest', but in most cases the context seems to require 'number of years' purchase'. *Fonds* is usually 'estate', but sometimes 'fund(s)'. *Laborieux* is rather difficult: sometimes it means 'occupied in work', sometimes 'arduous', and sometimes 'industrious', and the translation varies with the context. *Rente* can mean 'rent', 'unearned income', or 'annuity', and once again the translation varies with the context. *Travaux* is perhaps the most difficult word of all: sometimes it is translated as 'labour(s)', sometimes as 'work', and in a few places as 'manufactures' or 'industry'.

Special difficulties occur in the case of the names of the different groups engaged in agriculture. I have usually translated *laboureur* and *colon* as 'husbandman', *cultivateur* as 'cultivator', and *fermier* as 'farmer'. *Métayer* I have left in its original form. None of these equivalents is entirely satisfactory, but I have been unable to find better ones.[1]

A special note is required about *affecté*, which is used both in the sense of 'mortgaged', pledged', or 'encumbered', and in the sense of 'assigned to' or 'earmarked for'. When it is used in the latter sense, it means in effect that the person or thing 'assigned to' or 'earmarked for' some purpose cannot be interfered with or encroached upon without hindering the fulfilment of the purpose.

The most important – and interesting – difficulties, however, relate to the words *capital*, *entreprise* and *entreprise*, *fabrication* and *fabrique*, *industrie*, *manufacture*, *profit*, *salaire*, and *verser* and *reverser*. The point here is that Turgot, as the context shows, normally used these words in something very closely approaching the specifically *economic* sense in which they are used today, rather than in the broader and more general sense in which they had been more or less exclusively used up to his time. For Turgot, in most contexts at any rate, an *entreprise* was not merely a venture, or undertaking, but a specific kind of undertaking under the direction of a capitalist entrepreneur. *Profit* was not merely a benefit, or gain, but a specific kind of gain made by the owner of a capital. *Salaire* was not merely a recompense, or reward, but a specific kind of reward paid to the workers employed by an entrepreneur; and so on. Occasionally, of course, Turgot also uses these words in their more general sense, and one has to be careful not to make him out as more 'modern' than he actually was. But with Turgot one has fewer inhibitions than one does in the case of the Physiocrats about translating the words listed at the beginning of this paragraph as (in order) 'capital', 'entrepreneur' and 'enterprise', 'manufacture' and 'factory', 'industry', 'manufacture', 'profit', 'wage(s)', and 'invest' and 'reinvest'. That is how they have in fact usually been translated in the text below.

APPENDIX B: THE EARLY EDITIONS OF THE 'REFLECTIONS'

The most difficult problem which confronts a translator of Turgot's *Reflections* is that of the edition from which he should work. For reasons set out below, I have thought it proper to use as my basis the edition of 1788,[2] which, although

---

[1] See my *Economics of Physiocracy*, pp. 40–2, for comments on the translation of these words, and also certain others – notably *productif*, *produit net*, and *revenu*, which I have rendered simply as 'productive', 'net product', and 'revenue'.

[2] This edition, *Réflexions sur la Formation et la Distribution des Richesses. Par M. Turgot*, has no publisher's name or place of publication, and there is no evidence as to who might have been responsible for it. It bears the date 'M.DCC LXXXVIII' on the title-page, and '*Novembre 1766*' at the end of the text.

APPENDICES TO THE INTRODUCTION

apparently published seven years after Turgot's death, seems to me to be the one which is likely to approximate most closely to the original manuscript which Turgot sent to Du Pont in 1769 for publication in *Éphémérides*.

It is clear from Turgot's letter of 2 December 1769,[1] under cover of which he sent the manuscript, that the latter contained 101 'paragraphs' or sections, this being (as he put it) 'like 1001, the number consecrated to this kind of thing'. He told Du Pont that he had added marginal summaries which could be used as titles, and that he had also added a short preface which Du Pont could use or not, as he wished; and he asked for 100 or 150 offprints to be run off, including two (concerning which he gave detailed instructions) which could be used as working copies if and when he decided to 'make something passable' of the piece. On 12 January 1770 Turgot wrote a further letter to Du Pont, asking him (*inter alia*) to remove 'the theological part of the piece on usury', which he was making use of in another place;[2] and on January 30 he wrote to him again, referring once more to his use in another place of 'the discussion on the *mutuum date* passage'.[3]

By 2 February 1770, the date of Turgot's next extant letter to Du Pont, the November volume of *Éphémérides* for 1769 (no. 11) had at last appeared,[4] and Turgot had found, upon reading in it the first instalment of his *Reflections*, that Du Pont had taken a number of unwarrantable liberties with the text. In particular, he had added in XVII a clause to the effect that the right of property in land was the 'price of the *avances foncières*';[5] he had inserted in XXI a phrase containing the unduly Physiocratic expression '*lois de l'ordre*'; and he had expanded XXI into three separate sections, adding certain material of his own in the course of which he had claimed in effect that it could never be profitable for an individual to own slaves. In his letter of 2 February, Turgot demanded that Du Pont should conform to his manuscript in the remaining instalments, and that if the material had already been printed appropriate cancels[6] should be inserted. He also demanded that cancels should be inserted in the offprints he had asked for, in the three places where Du Pont had made unauthorised alterations, and that the eulogistic foreword which Du Pont had substituted for Turgot's own preface should be removed from them.[7] Du Pont duly promised that the offprints would be restored so as to conform to the manuscript,[8] but

[1] Schelle, III, pp. 73–4.
[2] Schelle, III, pp. 370–1. 'Besides', Turgot added, 'the matter is still in dispute.'
[3] Schelle, III, pp. 372–3. The '*mutuum date* passage' is discussed in LXXIII and LXXV.
[4] According to Schelle (III, p. 373, footnote *b*) it was not released by the censor until 23 January 1770.
[5] This was a particularly touchy point with Turgot: cf. Schelle, II, pp. 374, 378, and 379. On the substantive issue at stake, see L. Rogin, *The Meaning and Validity of Economic Theory* (New York, 1956), pp. 34–6.
[6] '*Cancel*' (*carton* in French) here means a reprinted leaf which is substituted for one which has been suppressed.
[7] Schelle, III, p. 374.
[8] Schelle, III, p. 379.

warned Turgot that he had made some other small 'corrections' in the *Éphémé-rides* version – apparently the insertion in the last sentence of XXXI, and possibly in the second sentence of LXVI, of a reference to the means of payment, to which Turgot objected only on the grounds that it was unnecessary in the context.[1]

By 2 March 1770, as is clear from another letter to Du Pont of that date,[2] Turgot had received the December volume of *Éphémérides* for 1769 (no. 12), in which the second instalment of the *Reflections* was published. Besides the 'corrections' relating to the means of payment, Du Pont had apparently made a further and more substantial 'correction' to LV and LVI,[3] but in his letter of 2 March Turgot made no reference to the latter. He reminded Du Pont, how-ever, of his desire that the 'theological part' of the discussion on usury in the final instalment should be cut out, and asked that the two offprints in the form of working copies, together with 'three or four others', should be sent to him.

By 23 March, the date of Turgot's next letter to Du Pont, the January volume of *Éphémérides* for 1970 (no. 1), containing the final instalment of the *Reflections*, had appeared. The two 'theological' sections (LXXIII and LXXV) had been duly removed, and no further 'corrections' of substance would seem to have been made, although Du Pont had added a long critical note to LXXVIII which attracted Turgot's scorn,[4] and shorter notes to LXXXI, LXXXVI, and XC. By 23 March, too, Turgot had apparently received a bundle of five or six offprints[5] and checked them. Under cover of his letter of 23 March he sent Du Pont an errata for the offprint, asking him if he could find someone who would neatly correct the most essential of the errors by hand. He also sent him instructions for three cancels, and a list of people to whom the final version of the offprint should be sent. In his next letter, dated 29 March, we find Turgot on the verge of sending another cancel, but changing his mind and sending instead a note of five addi-tional errors to be included in the errata.[6]

Given all these circumstances, it seems very likely that the final version of the offprint must have closely resembled the original manuscript, and that any divergences must have been made or at any rate implicitly authorised by Turgot himself. By the courtesy of Columbia University I have been able to obtain a microfilm of a document in their possession which bears all the marks of being a copy of the final version of the offprint. It contains 101 sections; there is no preface; the two 'theological' sections are reinstated;[7] the offending passages

---

[1] Schelle, III, pp. 378–9 and 381. The first of these 'corrections' was duly removed in the offprint, but the second was not.

[2] Schelle, III, pp. 380–2.

[3] He had suppressed the title of LV and the whole of its first sentence; removed the reference to slaves in the second sentence and substituted a reference to movable wealth; and run together the remainder of LV with LVI, making one section alone (instead of two), under the title of LVI.

[4] Schelle, III, pp. 383–4.

[5] Schelle, III, pp. 383, 385 and 387.

[6] Schelle, III, p. 386.

[7] We do not really know whether Turgot in fact wanted both LXXIII and LXXV, or only

about *avances foncières, lois de l'ordre*, and means of payment are omitted; XXI is all in one section, and LV and LVI are separated; there is a long errata at the end; and most of the errors noted in the errata have been corrected in the text in a neat hand. As if to clinch the matter, a handwritten inscription on the title-page indicates that this copy was presented by Turgot to Houdon, on the occasion when the latter was making his bust.[1] There would seem to be little doubt that the Columbia University document is in fact a copy of the final version of the offprint authorised by Turgot for distribution to a selected number of recipients in 1770.

Turning now to the 1788 edition, this was almost certainly based on the 1770 offprint. Most of the corrections indicated in the errata of the latter have been incorporated in the 1788 text, and although there is a large number of additional changes these are almost all relatively minor ones, consisting either of corrections of printer's errors, or of improvements in spelling, punctuation, and grammar. In three places a word or phrase has been omitted, but in each case this would seem to have been accidental. In three other places a word has been deliberately changed – *mitoyen* to *moyen* in XXXII, *éternellement* to *long-tems* in XLII, and *superflu* to *surplus* in C – but these are all intelligent changes which Turgot, even if he did not in fact make them himself, would probably not have disowned. It is at least possible that the 1788 edition was based on a copy of the 1770 offprint containing further corrections made by Turgot himself. At any rate it would seem justifiable to use the 1788 edition as the basis for a translation, and this is what I have done. Since the 1788 edition itself contains a number of printing errors, however – although not nearly as many as the 1770 offprint – I have on several occasions gone back to the latter in order to reproduce what I believe to have been the intended reading.

There is one final and rather tiresome matter concerning the numbering of the sections which requires to be cleared up. In the 1770 offprint there are two successive sections each numbered LXVI, and there is no section numbered LXXI. These two errors, which may well have occurred in the course of the insertion of Turgot's cancels, in effect neutralise one another, so that the last section is correctly numbered CI, as was (presumably) the last section of the original manuscript. In the 1788 edition the second of these errors is corrected but not the first, so that the last section is numbered C, giving the impression

the latter, removed from the *Éphémérides* version. Nor do we really know whether he in fact wanted these sections restored in the offprint: in a letter to Caillard (who was translating the work into German) dated 5 May 1774 (Schelle, III, pp. 674–6), Turgot asked him to delete LXXV. 'I asked Du Pont to delete it', Turgot wrote, 'but he did not want to throw away three pages of type.' What is certain, however, is that both LXXIII and LXXV were in the original manuscript; that Turgot asked Du Pont to conform to the original manuscript in the offprint; and that in 1770, when the offprint was produced, he authorised, or at any rate acquiesced in, the inclusion in it of LXXIII and LXXV.

[1] 'This bust is signed and dated 1778' (Schelle, V, p. 665).

that there are only 100 sections whereas there are in fact 101. In my translation I have corrected both the errors, renumbering the later sections accordingly. The numbering in the translation, therefore, in all probability conforms fairly exactly to that in Turgot's original manuscript.

A Philosophical Review of the Successive Advances
of the Human Mind

The phenomena of nature, governed as they are by constant laws, are confined within a circle of revolutions which are always the same. All things perish, and all things spring up again; and in these successive acts of generation through which plants and animals reproduce themselves time does no more than restore continually the counterpart of what it has caused to disappear.

The succession of mankind, on the other hand, affords from age to age an ever-changing spectacle. Reason, the passions, and liberty ceaselessly give rise to new events: all the ages are bound up with one another by a succession of causes and effects which link the present state of the world with all those that have preceded it. The arbitrary signs of speech and writing, by providing men with the means of securing the possession of their ideas and communicating them to others, have made of all the individual stores of knowledge a common treasure-house which one generation transmits to another, an inheritance which is always being enlarged by the discoveries of each age. Thus the human race, considered over the period since its origin, appears to the eye of a philosopher as one vast whole, which itself, like each individual, has its infancy and its advancement.

We see the establishment of societies, and the formation of nations which in turn dominate other nations or become subject to them. Empires rise and fall; laws and forms of government succeed one another; the arts and the sciences are in turn discovered and perfected, in turn retarded and accelerated in their progress; and they are passed on from country to country. Self-interest, ambition, and vainglory continually change the world scene and inundate the earth with blood; yet in the midst of their ravages manners are softened, the human mind becomes more enlightened, and separate nations are brought closer to one another. Finally commercial and political ties unite all parts of the globe, and the whole human race, through alternate periods of rest and unrest, of weal and woe, goes on advancing, although at a slow pace, towards greater perfection.

In the time placed at my disposal I could not hope to portray for you the whole of so vast a panorama. I shall try merely to indicate the main lines of the progress of the human mind; and this discourse will be wholly

41

taken up with some reflections on the origin and growth of the arts and sciences and the revolutions which have taken place in them, considered in their relation to the succession of historical events.

Holy Writ, after having enlightened us about the creation of the universe, the origin of man, and the birth of the first arts, before long puts before us a picture of the human race concentrated again in a single family as the result of a universal flood. Scarcely had it begun to make good its losses when the miraculous confusion of tongues forced men to separate from one another. The urgent need to procure subsistence for themselves in barren deserts, which provided nothing but wild beasts, obliged them to move apart from one another in all directions and hastened their diffusion through the whole world. Soon the original traditions were forgotten; and the nations, separated as they were by vast distances and still more by the diversity of languages, strangers to one another, were almost all plunged into the same barbarism in which we still see the Americans.

But natural resources and the fertile seeds of the sciences are to be found wherever there are men. The most exalted mental attainments are only and can only be a development or combination of the original ideas based on sensation, just as the building at whose great height we gaze in wonder necessarily has its foundation in the earth upon which we tread. The same senses, the same organs, and the spectacle of the same universe, have everywhere given men the same ideas, just as the same needs and inclinations have everywhere taught them the same arts.

Now a faint light begins occasionally to penetrate the darkness which has covered all the nations, and step by step it spreads. The inhabitants of Chaldea, closest to the source of the original traditions, the Egyptians, and the Chinese apparently lead the rest of the peoples. Others follow them at a distance, and progress leads to further progress. The inequality of nations increases; in one place the arts begin to emerge, while in another they advance at a rapid rate towards perfection. In some nations they are brought to a standstill in the midst of their mediocrity, while in others the original darkness is not yet dissipated at all. Thus the present state of the world, marked as it is by these infinite variations in inequality, spreads out before us at one and the same time all the gradations from barbarism to refinement, thereby revealing to us at a single glance, as it were, the records and remains of all the steps taken by the human mind, a reflection of all the stages through which it has passed, and the history of all the ages.

But is not nature everywhere the same? – and if she leads all men to the same truths, if even their errors are alike, how is it that they do not all move forward at the same rate along the road which is marked out for them? It is true that the human mind everywhere contains the potential for the same progress, but nature, distributing her gifts unequally, has given to certain minds an abundance of talents which she has refused to others. Circumstances either develop these talents or allow them to become buried in obscurity; and it is from the infinite variety of these circumstances that there springs the inequality in the progress of nations.

Barbarism makes all men equal; and in early times all those who are born with genius are faced with virtually the same obstacles and the same resources. Societies are established and expanded, however; national hatreds and ambition – or rather greed, the only ambition of barbarous peoples – cause war and devastation to increase; and conquests and revolutions mix up peoples, languages, and customs in a thousand different ways. Chains of mountains, great rivers and seas confine the dealings of peoples with one another, and consequently their intermingling, within fixed boundaries. This results in the formation of common languages which become a tie binding several nations together, so that all the nations of the world become divided as it were into a number of different classes. Tillage increases the permanence of settlements. It is able to feed more men than are employed in it, and thus imposes upon those whom it leaves idle the necessity of making themselves either useful or formidable to the cultivators. Hence towns, trade, the useful arts and accomplishments, the division of occupations, the differences in education, and the increased inequality in the conditions of life. Hence that leisure, by means of which genius, relieved of the burden of providing for primary necessities, emerges from the narrow sphere within which these necessities confine it and bends all its strength to the cultivation of the arts. Hence that more rapid and vigorous rate of advance of the human mind which carries along with it all parts of society and which in turn derives additional momentum from their perfection. The passions develop alongside genius; ambition gathers strength; politics lends it ever-widening perspectives; victories have more lasting results and create empires whose laws, customs, and government, influencing men's genius in different ways, become a kind of common education for the nations, producing between one nation and another the same sort of difference which education produces between one man and another.

United, divided, the one raised up on the other's ruins, empires rapidly succeed one another. The revolutions which they undergo cause them to run the whole gamut of possible states, and unite and disunite all the elements of the body politic. Like the ebb and flow of the tide, power passes from one nation to another, and, within the same nation, from the princes to the multitude and from the multitude to the princes. As the balance shifts, everything gradually gets nearer and nearer to an equilibrium, and in the course of time takes on a more settled and peaceful aspect. Ambition, when it forms great states from the remains of a host of small ones, itself sets limits to its own ravages. Wars no longer devastate anything but the frontiers of empires; the towns and the countryside begin to breathe the air of peace; the bonds of society unite a greater number of men; ideas come to be transmitted more promptly and more widely; and the advancement of arts, sciences, and manners progresses more rapidly. Like a storm which has agitated the waves of the sea, the evil which is inseparable from revolutions disappears: the good remains, and humanity perfects itself. Amidst this complex of different events, sometimes favourable, sometimes adverse, which because they act in opposite ways must in the long run nullify one another, genius ceaselessly asserts its influence. Nature, while distributing genius to only a few individuals, has nevertheless spread it out almost equally over the whole mass, and with time its effects become appreciable.

Genius, whose course is at first slow, unmarked, and buried in the general oblivion into which time precipitates human affairs, emerges from obscurity with them by means of the invention of *writing*. Priceless invention! – which seemed to give wings to those peoples who first possessed it, enabling them to outdistance other nations. Incomparable invention! – which rescues from the power of death the memory of great men and models of virtue, unites places and times, arrests fugitive thoughts and guarantees them a lasting existence, by means of which the creations, opinions, experiences, and discoveries of all ages are accumulated, to serve as a foundation and foothold for posterity in raising itself ever higher!

But what a spectacle the succession of men's opinions presents! I seek there for the progress of the human mind, and I find virtually nothing but the history of its errors. Why is its course, which is so sure from the very first steps in the field of mathematical studies, so unsteady in everything else, and so apt to go astray? Let us try to discover the reasons. In mathematics, the mind deduces one from another a chain of propositions, the truth of which consists only in their mutual dependence. It is not the same with the other sciences, where it is no longer from the intercomparison of ideas that truth is born, but from their conformity with a sequence of real facts. To discover and verify truth, it is no longer a question of establishing a small number of simple principles and then merely allowing the mind to be borne along by the current of their consequences. One must start from nature as it is, and from that infinite variety of effects which so many causes, counterbalanced one by the other, have combined to produce. Notions are no longer assemblages of ideas which the mind forms of its own accord and of whose range it has exact knowledge. Ideas emerge and are assembled in our minds almost without our knowing it; we are beset by the images of objects right from the cradle. Little by little we learn to distinguish between them, less by reference to what they are in themselves than by reference to their relation to our habits and needs. The signs of language impress themselves on the mind while it is still undeveloped. At first, through habit and imitation, they become attached to particular objects, but later they succeed in calling up more general notions. This chaotic blend of ideas and expressions grows and becomes more complex all the time; and when man starts to seek for truth he find himself in the midst of a labyrinth which he has entered blindfold. Should we be surprised at his errors?

Spectator of the universe, his senses show him the effects but leave him ignorant of the causes. And to examine effects in an endeavour to find their unknown cause is like trying to guess an enigma: we think of one or more possible key words and try them in turn until one is found which fulfils all the conditions.

The natural philosopher erects hypotheses, follows them through to their consequences, and brings them to bear upon the enigma of nature. He tries them out, so to speak, on the facts, just as one verifies a seal by applying it to its impression. Suppositions which are arrived at on the basis of a small number of poorly understood facts yield to suppositions which are less absurd, although no more true. Time, research, and chance result in the accumulation of observations, and unveil the hidden connections which link a number of phenomena together.

Ever restless, incapable of finding tranquillity elsewhere than in the truth, ever stimulated by the image of that truth which it believes to be within its grasp but which flies before it, the curiosity of man leads to a multiplication of the number of questions and debates, and obliges him to analyse ideas and facts in a manner which grows ever more exact and more profound. Mathematical truths, becoming from day to day more numerous and hence more fruitful, point the way to the development of hypotheses which are more far-reaching and more precise, and indicate new experiments which, in their turn, present new problems for mathematics to resolve. Thus the need perfects the tool; thus mathematics is sustained by natural philosophy, upon which it sheds its light; thus everything is bound together; thus, in spite of the diversity in their development, all the sciences render mutual aid to one another; thus, by feeling his way, by multiplying systems and draining them, as it were, of their errors, man at last attains to the understanding of a great number of truths.

What ridiculous opinions marked our first steps! How absurd were the causes which our fathers thought up to make sense of what they saw! What sad monuments they are to the weakness of the human mind! The senses constitute the unique source of our ideas: the whole power of our mental faculties is restricted to combining the ideas which they have received from the senses: hardly even can they form combinations of ideas of which the senses do not provide them with a model. Hence that almost irresistible tendency to judge of what one does not know by what one knows; hence those delusive analogies to which the first men in their immaturity abandoned themselves with so little thought; hence the monstrous aberrations of idolatry. Men, oblivious of the original traditions, when affected by sensible phenomena, imagined that all effects which were independent of their own action were produced by beings similar to them, but invisible and more powerful, whom they substituted for the Divinity. When they were contemplating nature, it was as if they fixed their gaze on the surface of a deep sea instead of on the sea-bed hidden by the waters, and saw there only their own reflection. All objects of nature had their gods, which, being created after the model of man, shared his attributes and vices. Throughout the world, superstition sanctified the caprices of the imagination; and the only true God, the only God worthy of adoration, was known only in one corner of the earth, by the people whom he had expressly chosen.

In this slow progression of opinions and errors, pursuing one another, I fancy that I see those first leaves, those sheaths which nature has given to the newly-growing stems of plants, issuing before them from the earth, and withering one by one as other sheaths come into existence, until at last the stem itself makes its appearance and is crowned with flowers and fruit – a symbol of late-emerging truth!

Woe betide those nations, then, in which the sciences, as the result of a blind zeal for them, are confined within the limits of existing knowledge in an attempt to stabilise them. It is for this reason that the regions which were the first to become enlightened are not those where the sciences have made the greatest progress. The respect for the new-born philosophy which the glamour of its novelty inspires in men tends to perpetuate the first opinions: the sectarian spirit comes to be attached to it. Such a spirit is natural for the first philosophers, because arrogance feeds on ignorance, because the less one knows the less one doubts, and because the less one has discovered the less one sees what remains to be discovered. In Egypt, and long after in the Indes, superstition, which made the dogmas of the ancient philosophy the patrimony of the priestly families, who by consecrating them enchained them and incorporated them in the dogmas of a false religion; in great Asia, political despotism, the result of the establishment of great empires during the centuries of barbarism; the civic despotism born of slavery and of the plurality of wives which is a consequence of it; the want of vigour on the part of princes; the prostration of their subjects; in China, the very care which the Emperors took to regulate research and to tie up the sciences with the political constitution of the state, held them back forever in mediocrity: these trunks which since their origin had been too productive of branches soon ceased to grow higher.

With the passing of time new peoples came into being. In the course of the unequal progress of nations, the civilised peoples, surrounded by barbarians, now conquering, now conquered, intermingled with them. Whether the latter received from the former their arts and their laws together with servitude, or whether as conquerors they yielded to the natural empire of reason and culture over brute force, the bounds of barbarism steadily retreated.

The Phoenicians, inhabitants of a barren coast, had made themselves the agents of exchanges between peoples. Their ships, spread out over the whole Mediterranean, began to reveal nation to nation.

Astronomy, navigation, and geography were perfected, one by means of the other. The coasts of Greece and Asia Minor came to be filled with Phoenician colonies. Colonies are like fruits which cling to the tree only until they have reached their maturity: once they had become self-sufficient they did what Carthage was to do later, and what America will one day do.

Out of the intermingling of these colonies, each independent of the others, with the ancient peoples of Greece and with the remnants of all the swarms of barbarians who had successively ravaged her, there arose the Greek nation, or rather that family of nations comprised of a large number of small peoples who were prevented from aggrandising themselves at one another's expense by the fact that they were all equally weak and by the nature of the terrain, which was broken up by mountains and sea, and who were intermingled, divided, and reunited in a thousand different ways by their associations, their public and private interests, their civil and national wars, their migrations, the reciprocal duties of colonies and metropolises, one language, customs, a common religion, trade, public games, and the Amphictyonic league. In the course of these revolutions, and by means of these manifold interminglings, there was formed that rich, expressive, and sonorous language, the language of all the arts.

Poetry, which is no more than the art of painting with words, and the perfection of which depends so greatly on the genius of the languages which it employs, assumed in Greece a grandeur which it had never previously known. It was no longer, as it had been with the first men, a succession of barbarous words chained to the beat of a rustic song and to the steps of a dance as uncouth as the riotous joy which it expressed. It had decked itself out in a harmony which was all its own. The ear, ever more difficult to please, had laid down stricter rules; and if the burden of these had become heavier, the new expressions, turns of phrase, and felicitous boldnesses of style, which had increased in proportion, lent greater strength to bear it.

Good taste had finally succeeded in outlawing those involved figures and elephantine metaphors which we object to in Oriental poetry.

In those countries of Asia where societies arrived earlier at a stable state, and where writers appeared earlier, languages became stabilised at a point nearer to their first origin, and as a result were marked by that high-flown style which is characteristic of a language in its first imperfect stage. Languages are the measure of men's ideas: thus in early times there were names only for the objects which were most familiar to the senses; and to express these imperfect ideas it was necessary to have recourse to metaphors. A word which is coined signifies nothing, so that one must try, by putting together the signs of the ideas which are nearest akin, to set the mind on the track of what one wishes to communicate to it. The imagination attempts to grasp the thread of a certain analogy which binds together our senses with their different objects. An imperfect or far-fetched analogy gives birth to those clumsy and abundant metaphors which necessity, more ingenious than fastidious, employs, which good taste disavows, of which the first languages are full, and of which even now etymologists find vestiges in the most cultivated.

Languages, which are necessarily used by all men, and thus often by men of genius, are always perfected over time, when they are not immobilised by written works which become a permanent standard by which to judge of their purity. The habitual use of the spoken word leads continually to new combinations of ideas, calls attention to new relationships between them and to new shades of meaning, and makes felt the need for new expressions. Moreover, through the migrations of peoples, languages blend with one another like rivers and are enriched by the coming together of several languages.

Thus the Greek language, formed by the intermingling of a greater number of languages, and stabilised later than those of Asia, unites together harmony, richness, and variety. Homer consummated its triumph, poured into it the treasures of his genius, and lifted it to the greatest heights by the harmonious character of his poetry, the charm of his expression, and the splendour of his images.

Following on this, liberty, which as the result of a revolution natural to small states came to be established in all cities on the ruins of the government of a single man, gave a new stimulus to the genius of the Greeks. The different forms of government into which the opposing passions of the powerful and the people turn by turn precipitated them, taught the legislators to compare and to weigh up all the different elements in society, and to find the proper equilibrium between their forces; while at the same time the combined quarrels and interests of so many ambitious, weak, and jealous neighbouring republics taught the states to fear one another, to keep constant watch on one another, and to counterbalance successes with leagues, and led at the same time to the perfecting of politics and the art of war.

It was only after several centuries that philosophers appeared in Greece – or rather it was only then that the study of philosophy became the business of particular thinkers and appeared sufficiently extensive in its scope to occupy them fully. Until then, the poets had been at the same time the only philosophers and the only historians. When men are ignorant it is easy to know everything. But ideas were not yet by any means clear enough. A sufficiently large number of facts was not available; the time of truth had not by any means arrived, and the systems of the Greek philosophers could not yet be anything but adroit. Their metaphysics, shaky on the most important truths and often superstitious or blasphemous, was scarcely more than a collection of poetic fables or a tissue of unintelligible words; and their natural philosophy itself was nothing but shallow metaphysics.

Morality, although still imperfect, was less affected by the infancy of reason. The recurring needs which constantly call men into society and force them to bow to its laws; that instinct, that feeling for the good and the honourable which Providence has graven on all our hearts, which

49

comes before reason, and which often seduces it in spite of itself, leads the philosophers of all ages to the same fundamental principles of the science of behaviour. Socrates guided his fellow-citizens along the path of virtue; Plato sowed this path with flowers; the charm of his eloquence beautified even his errors. Aristotle, the most wide-ranging, profound, and truly philosophical mind of all antiquity, was the first to carry the torch of exact analysis into the sphere of philosophy and the arts. Unveiling the principles of certitude and the springs of feeling, he subjected the development of reason and even the fire of genius to constant rules.

Happy centuries, in which all the fine arts spread their light on every side, and in which the passion of a noble emulation was swiftly transmitted from one city to another! Painting, sculpture, architecture, poetry, and history grew up everywhere at the same time, as we see in the expanse of a forest a thousand different trees springing up, growing, and being crowned together.

Athens, governed by the decrees of a multitude whose tumultuous waves the orators calmed or agitated at their pleasure; Athens, where Pericles had taught the leaders how to buy the state at the expense of the state itself, and how to dissipate its treasures in order to exempt themselves from giving an account of them; Athens, where the art of governing the people was the art of amusing them, the art of feasting their ears, their eyes, and their curiosity always greedy for novelties, with festivities, pleasures, and constant spectacles, Athens owed to the very vices of its government which made it succumb to Lacedaemon that eloquence, that taste, that magnificence, and that splendour in all the arts which have made it the model of nations.

While the Athenians, the Spartans, and the Thebans are in turn arrogating to themselves superiority over the other cities, the Macedonian power, unnoticed, like a river which overflows its banks, slowly extends into Greece under Philip, and violently inundates Asia under Alexander. This host of regions and states, from which the conquests of the Assyrians, the Medes, and the Persians, in successively swallowing one another up, had formed this great body, the product of so many conquerors and so many centuries, breaks up with a crash on the death of the conqueror of Darius. Wars between his generals establish new kingdoms; Syria and Egypt become a part of Greece, and receive the language, the customs, and the sciences of their conquerors.

Commerce and the arts render Alexandria the rival of Athens. Astronomy and the mathematical sciences are carried there to an even higher level than they have ever been before. Above all we see flourishing there

that erudition with which until then the Greeks had been little acquainted
– that kind of study which is concerned less with things than with books,
which consists less in producing and discovering than in assembling
together, comparing, and evaluating what has been produced and what
has been discovered; which does not move forward at all, but which
turns its gaze backwards in order to survey the road which has been
taken. The studies which demand the most genius are not always those
which imply the greatest progress in the mass of mankind. There are
minds to whom nature has given a memory which is capable of assembling
together a large number of pieces of knowledge, a power of exact reasoning which is capable of comparing them and arranging them in a manner
which puts them in their full light, but to whom at the same time she has
denied that fire of genius which invents and which opens up new roads
for itself. Created to unite past discoveries under one point of view, to
clarify and even to perfect them, if they are not torches which shine with
their own light, they are diamonds which brilliantly reflect a borrowed
light, but which total darkness would confound with the meanest
stones.

The known world, if I may put it like that, the commercial world, the
political world, had expanded as a result of the conquests of Alexander.
The dissensions of his successors began to present a vaster spectacle, and,
amid these clashes and these oscillations of the great powers, the little
cities of Greece, situated in the midst of them, often the arena of their
struggles and a prey to the ravages of all the parties, were no longer
conscious of anything but their weakness. Eloquence was no longer the
mainspring of politics: henceforth, degraded in the obscurity of the
schools by childish declamations, it lost its brilliance along with its
power.

But for several centuries already, Rome, in Italy as if in a world apart,
had been advancing by a continual succession of triumphs towards the
conquest of the world. Victorious over Carthage, she appeared suddenly
in the midst of the nations. Peoples trembled and were brought into subjection: the Romans, conquerors of Greece, became aware of a new
empire, that of intellect and learning. Their austere uncouthness was
tamed. Athens found disciples, and soon rivals, among her conquerors.
Cicero displayed, at the Capitol and on the rostrum, an eloquence
derived from the lessons of the Greeks, of which its enslaved masters no
longer knew anything but the rules. The Latin language, softened and
enriched, brought Africa, Spain, and Gaul under orderly government.
The boundaries of the civilised world were identical with those of the

Roman power, and two rival languages, Greek and Latin, shared it between them.

The laws of Rome, created to govern one city, sank under the burden of the whole world: Roman liberty was extinguished in waves of blood. Octavius alone finally gathered in the fruit of the civil strife. Cruel usurper, temperate prince, he gave tranquillity to the earth. His enlightened protection stimulated all the arts. Italy had a Homer, less productive than the first, but wiser, more equable, just as harmonious, and perhaps more perfect. Sublimity, reason, and the graces united to create Horace. Taste was perfected in every sphere.

Knowledge of nature and of truth is as infinite as they are: the arts, whose aim is to please us, are as limited as we are. Time constantly brings to light new discoveries in the sciences; but poetry, painting, and music have a fixed limit which the genius of languages, the imitation of nature, and the limited sensibility of our organs determine, which they attain by slow steps and which they cannot surpass. The great men of the Augustan age reached it, and are still our models.

From this time until the fall of the Empire, we see nothing but a general decadence in which everything is plunged. Do men raise themselves up, then, only to fall? A thousand causes combine to deprave taste more and more: tyranny, which degrades minds below all things which are great; blind luxury, which, born of vanity, and judging works of art less as objects of taste than as symbols of opulence, is as opposed to their perfection as a civilised love of magnificence is favourable to it; enthusiasm for new things among those who, not having enough genius to invent them, only too often have enough wit to spoil the old; the imitation of the vices of great men and even the misplaced imitation of their beauties. Writers proliferate in the provinces and corrupt the language: I know not what remnants of the old Greek philosophy, mixed up with oriental superstitions, confounded with a host of empty allegories and magical spells, take possession of men's minds and smother the healthy natural philosophy which was beginning to spring up in the writings of Seneca and Pliny the Elder.

Soon the Empire, abandoned to the caprices of an insolent militia, becomes the prey of a host of tyrants, who, in the process of seizing it from one another, bring desolation and havoc to the provinces. Military discipline is destroyed, the northern barbarians penetrate on every side, peoples fall upon peoples, the cities become deserted, the fields are left uncultivated, and the western Empire, weakened by the transference of all its power to Constantinople, ruined everywhere by so many repeated ravages, at last suddenly collapses, and the Burgundians, Goths, and Franks are left to quarrel over its far-flung ruins and to found kingdoms in the different countries of Europe.

Could it be, in this sanctuary, that I should pass over in silence that new light which, while the Empire was proceeding towards its ruin, had spread out over the world – a light a thousand times more precious than those of letters and philosophy? Holy religion, could it be that I should forget you? Could I forget the perfecting of manners, the dissipation at last of the darkness of idolatry, and the enlightenment of men on the subject of the Divinity! Amid the almost total ruin of letters, you alone still created writers who were animated by the desire to instruct the faithful or to repel the attacks of the enemies of the faith; and when Europe fell prey to the barbarians, you alone tamed their ferocity; you alone have perpetuated the knowledge of the discarded Latin tongue; you alone have transmitted to us across so many centuries the minds, so to speak, of so many great men which had been entrusted to that language; and the conservation of the treasure of human knowledge, which was about to be dissipated, is one of your benefactions.

But the wounds of the human race were too deep; centuries were necessary to heal them. If Rome had been conquered by one people alone, their leader would have become a Roman, and his nation would have been absorbed in the Empire together with its language. We would have seen what the history of the world presents to us more than once: the spectacle of a civilised people invaded by barbarians, communicating to them its manners, its language, and its knowledge, and forcing them to make one people with it. Cicero and Virgil would have sustained the Latin language, just as Homer, Plato, and Demosthenes had defended theirs against the Roman power. But too many peoples, and too many ravages, succeeded one another; too many layers of barbarism were added one after the other before the first had time to disappear and yield to the force of the Roman sciences. Too many conquerors, too single-mindedly devoted to war, were for several centuries too much occupied with their quarrels. The genius of the Romans was extinguished and their language was lost, confounded with the Germanic languages.

It is a consequence of the intermingling of two languages that a new one is formed from them which is different from each; but a long time passes before they can be combined in a really intimate manner. Memory, wavering between the two, decides at random between the expressions of one and the other. Analogy, that is, the art of forming conjugations and declensions, of expressing the relationships between objects, and of arranging the expressions in discourse, has no longer any fixed rules. Ideas are associated in a confused manner; there is no longer any harmony or clarity in the language. Pour two liquids into the same vessel: you will see them become turbid and cloudy, and not recover the transparency they had when they were separate until time has rendered their mixture more intimate and more homogeneous. Thus, until a long succession of centuries has succeeded in giving the new language a uniform quality of its own, poetry, eloquence, and taste disappear almost completely. Thus new languages grew up in Europe, and in the chaos of their first formation ignorance and vulgarity ruled everywhere.

Unhappy empire of the Caesars, must new misfortunes be visited even upon those remnants which have escaped from thy wreck! Must it be that barbarism destroys at once all the refuges of the arts! And thou too, Greece, thine honours are then eclipsed! Finally the north seems to become exhausted, and new storms gather in the south against the only provinces which are not yet groaning under a foreign yoke!

The standard of a false prophet unites the wandering shepherds in the Arabian deserts; in less than a century Syria, Persia, Egypt, and Africa are covered by a raging torrent which ravages the whole territory from the Indian frontiers to the Atlantic Ocean and the Pyrenees. The Greek empire, confined within narrow boundaries, devastated in the south by the Saracens and then by the Turks, and in the north by the Bulgarians, laid waste internally by factions and by the instability of its throne, falls into a state of weakness and lethargy, and the cultivation of letters and arts ceases to occupy a debased, slack, and indolent populace.

In vain does Charlemagne in the west try to revive a few sparks of a fire which is buried under the ashes; their glow is as evanescent as it is feeble. Soon the quarrels of his grandsons disturb his empire; the north once again raises and sends forth new destroyers; the Normans and the Hungarians once again cover Europe with new ruins and a new darkness. Amid the general weakness, a new form of government puts the finishing touch to the ruin: the annihilated royal power gives way to that host of small sovereignties, subordinate one to another, among which the feudal laws maintain I know not what false semblance of order in the midst of the very anarchy which they perpetuate.

The kings without any authority, the nobles without any constraint, the peoples enslaved, the countryside covered with fortresses and ceaselessly ravaged, wars kindled between city and city, village and village, pene-trating, so to speak, the whole mass of the kingdoms; all commerce and all communications cut off; the towns inhabited by poor artisans enjoying no leisure; the only wealth and the only leisure which some men still enjoy lost in the idleness of a nobility scattered here and there in their castles who do nothing but engage in battles which are useless to the fatherland; the grossest ignorance extending over all nations and all occupations! An unhappy picture – but one which was only too true of Europe for several centuries!

But nevertheless, from the midst of this barbarism, perfected arts and sciences will one day rise again. Amid all the ignorance, progress is imperceptibly taking place and preparing for the brilliant achievements of later centuries; beneath this soil the feeble roots of a far-off harvest are already developing. The towns among all civilised peoples constitute by their very nature the centres of trade and the backbone of society. They continued to exist; and if the spirit of feudal government, born of the ancient customs of Germany, combined with a number of accidental circumstances, had abased them, this was a contradiction in the constitution of states which was bound to disappear in the long run. Soon we see the towns revive again under the protection of the princes; and the latter, in holding out their hands to the oppressed peoples, reduce the power of their vassals and little by little re-establish their own.

Latin and theology were already being studied in the universities, together with the Aristotelian dialectic. For a long time the Mussulman Arabs had been teaching themselves Greek philosophy, and their learning was spreading to the west. Mathematics had been extended as a result of their work. More independent than the other sciences of the perfection of taste and perhaps even of precision of intellect, one cannot study mathematics without being led to the truth. Always certain, always pure, its truths were emerging, encompassed about by the errors of judicial astrology. The chimerical search for the philosopher's stone, by encouraging the Arab philosophers to separate and to recombine all the elements of bodies, had led to the blossoming under their hands of the vast science of chemistry, and had spread it to all places where men were capable of being imposed upon by their greedy desires. Finally, on all sides, the mechanical arts were coming to be perfected by virtue of the simple fact that time was passing, because even in the decline of the sciences and taste the needs of life preserve them, and because, consequently, among that host of artisans who successively cultivate them it is impossible not to meet every now and then with one of those men of genius who are blended with the rest of mankind as gold is blended with the clay in a mine.

As a result, what a host of inventions unknown to the ancients and standing to the credit of these barbarous ages! Our art of musical notation, our bills of exchange, our paper, window glass, plate glass, windmills, clocks, spectacles, gunpowder, the magnetic needle, and the perfection of navigation and commerce. The arts are nothing but the utilisation of nature, and the practice of the arts is a succession of physical experiments which progressively unveil nature. Facts were accumulating in the darkness of the times of ignorance, and the sciences, whose progress although hidden was no less real, were bound to reappear one day augmented by this new wealth, like those rivers which after disappearing from our view for some time in a subterranean passage, reappear further on swollen by all the waters which have seeped through the earth.

Different series of events take place in different countries of the world, and all of them, as if by so many separate paths, at length come together to contribute to the same end, to raise up once again the ruins of the human spirit. Thus, in the night, we see the stars rise one after the other; they move forward, each in its own orbit; they seem in their common revolution to bear along with them the whole celestial sphere, and to bring in for us the day which follows them. Germany, Denmark, Sweden, and Poland through the efforts of Charlemagne and the Othos, and Russia through trade with the Greek empire, cease to be uncultivated forests. Christianity, in bringing together these scattered savages, in settling them in towns, is going to dry up forever the source of those inundations which have so often been fatal to the sciences. Europe is still barbarous; but the knowledge brought by her to even more barbarous peoples represents for them immense progress. Little by little the customs introduced by Germany into the south of Europe disappear. The nations, amid the quarrels of the nobles and the princes, begin to fashion for themselves the principles of a more stable government, and to acquire, in accordance with the different circumstances in which they find themselves, the particular character which distinguishes them. The wars against the Mussulmans in Palestine, by giving a common interest to all Christian states, teach them to know one another and to unite with one another, and sow the seeds of that modern political state of affairs in which so many nations seem to comprise nothing but one vast republic. Already we see the royal authority reviving again in France; the power of the people establishing itself in England; the Italian towns constituting themselves into republics and presenting the likeness of ancient Greece; the little monarchies of Spain driving the Moors before them and little by little joining up again into one whole. Soon the seas, which have hitherto separated the nations, come to be the link between them through the invention of the compass. The Portuguese in the east and the Spaniards in the west discover new worlds: at last the world as a whole is known.

Already the intermingling of the barbarous languages with Latin has during the course of the centuries produced new languages, of which the Italian, less removed from their common source and less mixed with foreign languages, takes precedence in the elegance of its style and the beauties of its poetry. The Ottomans, spreading through Asia and Europe with the swiftness of a violent wind, end by overthrowing the empire of Constantinople, and disseminate in the west the feeble sparks of those sciences which Greece still preserved.

What new art is suddenly born, as if to wing to every corner of the earth the writings and glory of the great men who are to come? How slow in every sphere is even the least progress! For two thousand years medals have presented to all eyes characters impressed upon bronze – and then, after so many centuries, some obscure individual realises that they can be impressed upon paper. At once the treasures of antiquity, rescued from the dust, pass into all hands, penetrate to every part of the world, bear light to the talents which were being wasted in ignorance, and summon genius from the depths of its retreats.

The time has come. Issue forth, Europe, from the darkness which covered thee! Immortal names of the Medici, of Leo X, of Francis I, be consecrated for ever! May the patrons of the arts share the glory of those who cultivate them! I salute thee, O Italy! – happy land, for the second time the homeland of letters and of taste, the spring from which their waters have spread to fertilise our territories. Our own France still only beholds thy progress from afar. Her language, still tainted by remnants of barbarism, cannot follow it. Soon fatal discords will rend the whole of Europe; audacious men have shaken the foundations of the faith and those of the empires; do the flowered stems of the fine arts grow when they are watered with blood? A day will come, and it is not far off, when they will beautify all the countries of Europe.

Time, spread your swift wings! Century of Louis, century of great men, century of reason, hasten! Already, even amidst the turmoil of heresy, the long-disturbed fortunes of states have ended by settling down, as if as the result of a final shock. Already the unremitting study of antiquity has brought men's minds back again to the point where its progress was arrested; already that host of facts, experiments, instruments, and ingenious exercises which the practice of the arts has accumulated over so many centuries, has been rescued from obscurity through printing; already the productions of the two worlds, brought together before our eyes as the result of a far-flung commerce, have become the foundation of a natural philosophy hitherto unknown, and freed at last from alien speculations; already on every hand attentive eyes are fixed upon nature: the remotest chances, turned to profit, give birth to discoveries. The son of an artisan in Zealand brings together for amusement two convex glasses in a tube; the boundaries of our senses are made to recede, and in Italy the eyes of Galileo have discovered a new firmament. Already Kepler, seeking in the stars for the numbers of Pythagoras, has discovered those two famous laws of the movements of the planets which one day in the hands of Newton will become the key to the universe. Already Bacon has traced out for posterity the road which it must follow.

Who is the mortal who dares to reject the learning of all the ages, and even those notions which he has believed to be the most certain? He seems to wish to extinguish the torch of the sciences in order to relight it all on his own at the pure fire of reason. Does he wish to imitate those peoples of antiquity among whom it was a crime to light at other fires that which was made to burn on the altars of the Gods? Great Descartes, if it was not always given to you to find the truth, at least you have destroyed the tyranny of error.

France, whom Spain and England have already outstripped in the glory of poetry; France, whose genius finishes forming itself only when the philosophical spirit begins to spread, will owe perhaps to this very backwardness the exactitude, the method, and the austere taste of her writers. Rarefied and affected thoughts, and the ponderous display of an ostentatious erudition, still corrupt our literature: a strange difference between our progress in taste and that of the ancients! The real advancement of the human mind reveals itself even in its aberrations; the caprices of Gothic architecture are never found among those who possess nothing but wooden huts. The acquisition of knowledge among the first men and the formation of taste kept pace, as it were, with one another. Hence a crude severity and an exaggerated simplicity were their prerogative. Guided by instinct and imagination, they seized little by little upon those relations between men and the objects of nature which are the sole foundations of the beautiful. In later times, when, in spite of the imperfection of taste, the number of ideas and perceptions was increased, when the study of models and rules had caused nature and feeling to become lost from men's view, it was necessary for them through reflection to take themselves back to where the first men had been led by blind instinct. And who is not aware that it is here that the supreme effort of reason lies?

At last all the shadows are dispelled: and what a light shines out on all sides! What a host of great men in every sphere! What a perfection of human reason! One man, Newton, has subjected the infinite to the calculus, has revealed the properties of light which in illuminating everything seemed to conceal itself, and has put into his balance the stars, the earth, and all the forces of nature. And this man has found a rival. Leibnitz encompasses within his vast intellect all the objects of the human mind. The different sciences, confined at first to a small number of simple notions common to all, can no longer, when as a result of their progress they have become more extensive and more difficult, be envisaged otherwise than separately; but greater progress once again unites them, because there is discovered that mutual dependence of all truths which in linking them together illuminates each through the other; because, if each day adds to the vast extent of the sciences, each day also makes them easier, because methods are multiplied with discoveries, because the scaffolding rises with the building.

O Louis, what majesty surrounds thee! What splendour thy beneficent hand has spread over all the arts! Thine happy people has become the centre of refinement! Rivals of Sophocles, of Menander, and of Horace, gather around his throne! Arise, learned academies, and unite your efforts for the glory of his reign! What a multitude of public monuments, of works of genius, of arts newly invented, and of old arts perfected! Who could possibly picture them? Open your eyes and see! Century of Louis the Great, may your light beautify the precious reign of his successor! May it last for ever, may it extend over the whole world! May men continually make new steps along the road of truth! Rather still, may they continually become better and happier!

In the midst of these vicissitudes of opinions, of sciences, of arts, and of everything which is human, rejoice, gentlemen, in the pleasure of seeing that religion to which you have consecrated your hearts and your talents, always true to herself, always pure, always complete, standing perpetuated in the Church, and preserving all the features of the seal which the Divinity has stamped upon it. You will be her ministers, and you will be worthy of her. The Faculty expects from you her glory, the Church of France her illumination, Religion her defenders. Genius, learning, and piety are united to give ground for their hopes.

On Universal History

༄༅

CONTENTS

Prefatory Note by Du Pont

M. Turgot rendered to Bossuet the homage which the loftiness of his thought and the energy of his expression deserve. He admired the noble and rapid flow of his style, its wealth of expression, its grandeur, and its harmonious dignity. But after having paid this tribute to his excellence as a writer, he regretted that his *Discourse on Universal History* was not more rich in insights, in reason, and in true perceptions. It was with sorrow that he saw it as not living up to the high-minded design of the author, to the interesting position in which he found himself as the tutor of a king, and to the majestic talent which no other French orator has yet equalled.

Nevertheless it was not in M. Turgot's nature to disparage a celebrated work and to slight a great man.

He preferred to rewrite the book, to give it the far-reaching scope which he would have wished it to have, and to embody in it principles which the illustrious Bishop of Meaux had passed over in silence, had not perhaps conceived, and would not perhaps have accepted.

Such a work could not be executed at one stroke. M. Turgot therefore judged it proper, before undertaking it, to sketch out a plan of it, not limiting himself to a bald and simple list of the subjects which he wanted to write about and develop, but delineating them with strokes of a brush as great artists do in their skilful outlines of a portrait.

This plan was not completed, but we have found the first sketch of it, which we are reproducing here.

The work is unfinished, but not one of its pages could have been written by a man who had not conceived it in its entirety, and who had not considered with deep attention and in all their aspects the multitude of subjects which it was to encompass.

❧⁂❧

PLAN OF THE DISCOURSES ON UNIVERSAL HISTORY

Idea of the Introduction

Set by his Creator in the midst of eternity and immensity, and occupying in them but one point, man necessarily enters into relations with a multitude of things and beings, while at the same time his ideas are concentrated in the indivisibility of his mind and of the present moment. He knows himself only through his sensations, which all have reference to external objects, and the present moment is a centre at which a host of interlinked ideas converge.

It is from this interlinking, and from the order of the laws which all these ideas follow in their continual variations, that man acquires the consciousness of reality. Through the relation of all his different sensations he becomes aware of the existence of external objects. A similar relation in the succession of his ideas reveals the past to him. The relations of beings with one another are by no means passive relations. All may act on one another according to their different laws, and also according to their distances from one another. This real world, of whose limits we are ignorant, has for us very narrow ones, which depend more or less on the perfection of our senses. We have knowledge of a small number of links in the chain, but the extremities in the great and the small equally escape us.

The laws governing bodies constitute physics: always constant, they are described, not recounted. The history of animals, and above all that of men, presents quite a different spectacle. Men, like animals, succeed to other men to whom they owe their existence, and they see, as animals do, their fellows spread out over the surface of the globe which they inhabit. But, being endowed with a more developed reason and more liberty of action, man's relations with his fellows are much more numerous and varied. Possessor of the treasure-house of signs, which he has had the ability to multiply almost to infinity, he can assure himself of the possession of all his acquired ideas, communicate them to other men, and transmit them to his successors as a heritage which is always being augmented. A continual combination of this progress with the passions, and with the events they have caused, constitutes the history of the human race, in which each man is no more than one part of an immense whole which has, like him, its infancy and its advancement.

Thus Universal History encompasses a consideration of the successive advances of the human race, and the elaboration of the causes which have contributed to it; the early beginnings of mankind; the formation and intermingling of nations; the origin of governments and their revolutions; the progress of languages, of natural philosophy, of morals, of manners, of the arts and sciences; the revolutions which have brought about the succession of empire to empire, of nation to nation, and of religion to religion; the human race always remaining the same during these upheavals, like the water of the sea during storms, and always proceeding towards its perfection. To unveil the influence of general and necessary causes, that of particular causes and the free actions of great men, and the relation of all this to the very constitution of man; to reveal the springs and mechanisms of moral causes through their effects – that is what History is in the eyes of a philosopher. It is based upon geography and chronology, which measure the distances between times and places.

In presenting, according to this plan, a picture of the human race, following roughly the historical order of its progress and laying stress on the main epochs, I do not want to go into things deeply but only to give an outline, a mere sketch of a great study, and to afford a glimpse of a vast arena without traversing it; just as we see through a narrow window all the immensity of the heavens.

PLAN OF THE FIRST DISCOURSE

On the Formation of Governments and the Intermingling of Nations

The whole universe proclaims to us a supreme Being. Everywhere we see the print of the hand of a GOD.

If we want to arrive at a knowledge of something more precise, we are surrounded by mists.

Every day we see arts invented; in some parts of the world we see peoples who are civilised and enlightened, and in other parts nomadic peoples in the depths of the forests. In an eternity of time this inequality of progress would have been bound to disappear. Thus the world is not eternal; but we are bound at the same time to conclude that it is very old. Just how old? We do not know.

Historical times cannot be traced further back than the invention of writing; and, when it was invented, men could at first make use of it only to record vague traditions, or a few leading events to which no dates were ascribed, and which were mixed up with myths to such an extent as to render discrimination impossible.

The pride of nations has led them to shift their origins far back into the depths of antiquity. But in relation to time, men, before the invention of numbers, could scarcely have extended their ideas beyond the few generations with which they were acquainted, that is, three or four. It is only within a century or a century and a half that tradition, unaided by history, can indicate the period of a known event. Thus no history can be traced much further back than the invention of writing, unless it be by means of a mythical chronology, which men took the trouble to create only when nations, revealed to one another through their commerce, had converted their pride into jealousy.

In this silence of reason and history, a book has been given to us as a repository of revelation. It tells us that this world has existed for six thousand or eight thousand years (according to the different copies); that we all owe our origin to a single man and a single woman; that it was through the punishment of their disobedience that man, born for a happier state, was reduced to a degree of ignorance and poverty which he was able partly to dispel only by means of time and labour. It deftly sketches out for us the invention of the first arts, the fruit of men's first needs, and the succession of generations, up to the point at which the human race, almost completely engulfed by a universal flood, was once again reduced to a single family, and thus obliged to start afresh.

This book, then, does not by any means stand between us and what we are looking for – the way in which men have come to be spread out over the earth, and political societies to be organised. It offers a new point of departure for these significant events, similar to that which would have been adopted even if the facts which it relates to us had not become an article of our faith.

Without provisions, and in the depths of forests, men could devote themselves to nothing but obtaining their subsistence. The fruits which the earth produces in the absence of cultivation are not enough: men had to resort to the hunting of animals, which, being limited in number and incapable in a given region of providing many men with food, have for this very reason accelerated the dispersion of peoples and their rapid diffusion.

Families or small nations widely separated from one another, because each required a very large area to obtain its food: that was the state of hunters. They have no fixed dwelling-place at all, and move extremely easily from one spot to another. Difficulty in getting a living, a quarrel, or the fear of an enemy are enough to separate families of hunters from the rest of their nation.

So they move aimlessly wherever the hunt leads them. And if another hunt leads them further in the same direction, their separation from one another increases. Thus peoples who speak the same language sometimes find themselves at distances of more than 600 leagues from one another, and surrounded by peoples who do not understand them. This is common among the savages of America, where we see, for the same reason, nations of fifteen or twenty men.

It is nevertheless not rare to find that wars and quarrels, motives for which barbarous peoples are only too clever at thinking up, have brought about interminglings which out of a large number of nations have sometimes formed one single nation through a general similarity of customs, and of languages which are distinguished from one another only by a large number of dialects.

The custom among the savages of America of adopting their prisoners of war in place of the men whom they lose in their expeditions must have made these interminglings very frequent. We see languages holding sway over vast stretches of country, such as that of the Hurons in the vicinity of the St Lawrence river, that of the Algonkins extending down to the Mississippi, that of the Mexicans, that of the Incas, that of the Topinambours in Brazil, and that of the Guaranis in Paraguay. The boundaries between them are commonly great mountain ranges.

There are animals which allow themselves to be brought into subjection by men, such as oxen, sheep, and horses, and men find it more advantageous to gather them together into herds than to chase after wandering animals.

It did not take long for the pastoral way of life to be introduced in all places where these animals were met with: oxen and sheep in Europe, camels and goats in the east, horses in Tartary, and reindeer in the north.

The way of life of hunting peoples is maintained in the parts of America where these species are lacking. In Peru, where nature has placed a species of sheep called *llamas*, the people are shepherds, and this is obviously the reason why that part of America has been more easily civilised.

Pastoral peoples, whose subsistence is more abundant and more assured, were the most numerous. They began to grow richer, and to understand better the idea of property. Ambition, or rather greed, which is the ambition of barbarians, was able to inspire them with the inclination to plunder, and at the same time with the will and the courage to hold their own. Tending herds involved trouble from which hunters were free, and herds sustained more men than were required to look after them. Thus a disproportion was bound to arise between the quickness of movement of the disposable population and that of the nation. Thus a nation could not shun the fight against a horde of determined men, whether hunters or even members of other pastoral nations, who would remain masters of the herds if they became conquerors, but who were also sometimes repelled by the cavalry of the shepherds, if the herds of the latter consisted of horses or camels. And as the conquered could not flee without dying of hunger, they shared the fate of the beasts and became the slaves of the conquerors, whom they sustained by tending their herds. The masters, relieved of all these cares, for their part went on subjecting others in the same manner. Thus small nations were formed which in their turn formed large ones. So these peoples spread out over a whole continent, until they were stopped by what appeared to be impenetrable barriers.

The incursions of pastoral peoples leave more traces than those of hunters. Susceptible to a greater number of desires, as a result of the idleness which they enjoyed, they went rushing to wherever they hoped to find booty and seized hold of it. They remained wherever they found pasturage, and intermingled with the inhabitants of the country.

The example of the first encouraged others. The course of these torrents widened, with peoples and languages constantly intermingling.

But these conquerors soon disappeared. When there was nothing left to pillage, the various hordes had no further interest in remaining together, and, besides, the multiplication of herds forced them to separate. Each horde had its chief. But some principal chief, or one who was more warlike, would retain a certain superiority over the others throughout his nation, and would exact from them various gifts as tokens of homage.

At last false ideas of glory entered the picture. What had formerly been done for the purpose of pillage was now done in order to exercise domination, to raise their own nation above others; and, when trade between peoples had made them acquainted with the attributes of different foreign countries, to exchange a barren country for a fertile one.

Every prince who was in any way ambitious made raids on the lands of his neighbours, and extended his power until he encountered someone capable of resisting him; then there was a battle; and the conqueror added the power of the conquered to his own and made use of it for new conquests.

Hence all those inundations of barbarians which have so often ravaged the earth – those ebbs and flows which constitute their whole history.

Hence those different names which peoples of the same country have successively borne, the variety of which confounds the researches of scholars. The name of the dominant nation became the general name for all the others, which nevertheless kept their particular names. Such were the Medes, the Persians, the Celts, the Teutons, the Cimbri, the Suevians, the Germans, the Allemands, the Scythians, the Getae, the Huns, the Turks, the Tartars, the Mogols, the Manchurians, the Kalmucks, the Arabs, the Bedouins, the Berbers, etc.

All conquests were not equally extensive; barriers which would not have stopped a hundred thousand men would stop ten thousand; thus a much greater number of small conquests took place within countries which were cut off. Revolutions were bound to be much more frequent there, and more intermingling of nations was bound to occur. Rivers, and to an even greater extent mountain ranges and the sea, formed impenetrable barriers for a great number of these would-be Attilas. Thus, in between the mountain ranges, the rivers, and the seas, small scattered peoples were reunited, fused together by the multiplicity of revolutions. Their languages and their customs were intimately blended together to assume, as it were, a uniform colour.

Beyond these first natural barriers, conquests were more extensive and interminglings less frequent.

Particular customs and dialects form different nations. All obstacles that diminish communication, and consequently distance, which is one of these obstacles, heighten the distinctions which separate nations; but in general the peoples of one continent are mingled together, at any rate indirectly: the Gauls with the Germans, the latter with the Sarmatians, and so on as far as it is possible to go so long as great seas do not separate them. Hence those customs and those words which are common to peoples very distant and very different from one another. Languages, customs, and even human forms seem to me like coloured bands running across all the nations of a continent in all directions and forming a succession of perceptible gradations, each nation being tinged with a shade intermediate between those of the nations which neighbour it. Sometimes all the nations are blended together; sometimes one transmits to another what it has itself received. But almost all these revolutions are unknown to history; they leave no more traces than storms do on the sea. It is only when their course has encompassed civilised peoples that the memory of them is preserved.

Pastoral peoples in fertile countries were no doubt the first to move on to the state of agriculture. Hunting peoples, who are deprived of the assistance of animals to manure the soil and to facilitate labour, were unable to arrive so soon at agriculture. If they cultivate any land at all, it is only a small quantity; when it is exhausted they move their habitation elsewhere; and if they are able to abandon their nomadic life it is only by infinitely slow steps.

Husbandmen are not by nature conquerors; the cultivation of the land keeps them too busy. But, being more wealthy than the other peoples, they were obliged to defend themselves against violence. Besides, with them the land can sustain many more men than are necessary in order to cultivate it. Hence people who are unoccupied; hence towns, trade, and all the useful arts and accomplishments; hence more rapid progress in every sphere, for everything follows the general advancement of the mind; hence greater skill in war than in the case of barbarians; hence the division of occupations and the inequality of men; hence slavery in domestic form, and the subjection of the weaker sex (always bound up with barbarism), the hardship of which increases in proportion to the increase in wealth. But at the same time a more searching enquiry into government begins.

The inhabitants of the cities, who were cleverer than those of the countryside, brought the latter into subjection; or, rather, a village which by means of its situation had become a convenient centre where the neighbouring population gathered for purposes of trade, and which had a larger number of people, became the dominant one, and, leaving in the other villages only those who were necessary for the cultivation of the land, drew to itself, either by means of slavery or through the attraction of government and commerce, the largest number of inhabitants. The blending together and union of the different departments of government became more intimate and more stable. And in the leisure of the cities, the passions were developed alongside genius.

Ambition gathered strength, politics lent it perspectives, and the progress of the mind enlarged them: hence a thousand different forms of government. The first were necessarily the product of war, and thus implied government by one man alone. We need not believe that men ever voluntarily gave themselves *one master*; but they have often agreed in recognising *one chief*. And the ambitious themselves, in forming great nations, have contributed to the designs of Providence, to the progress of enlightenment, and thus to the increase in the happiness of the human race, with which they were not concerned at all. Their passions, even their fits of rage, have led them on their way without their being aware of where they were going. I seem to see a huge army, every movement of which is directed by some mighty genius. When the military signals are given, when the trumpets sound tumultuously and the drums beat, whole squadrons of cavalry move off, the very horses are filled with a passion which has no aim, and each part of the army makes its way through the obstacles without knowing what may result from it: the leader alone sees the combined effect of all these different movements. Thus the passions have led to the multiplication of ideas, the extension of knowledge, and the perfection of the mind, in the absence of that reason whose day had not yet come and which would have been less powerful if its reign had arrived earlier.

Reason, which is justice itself, would not have taken away from anyone what belonged to him, would have banished wars and usurpations for ever, and would have left men divided up into a host of nations separated from one another and speaking different languages. As a result the human race, limited in its ideas, incapable of that progress in all kinds of under-standing, and in the sciences, arts, and government, which takes its rise from the collective genius of different regions, would have remained for ever in a state of mediocrity. Reason and justice, if they had been more attended to, would have immobilised everything, as has virtually hap-pened in China. But what is never perfect ought never to be entirely immobilised. The passions, tumultuous and dangerous as they are, became a mainspring of action and consequently of progress; everything which draws men away from their present condition, and everything which puts varied scenes before their eyes, extends the scope of their ideas, enlightens them, stimulates them, and in the long run leads them to the good and the true, towards which they are drawn by their natural bent. It is like the wheat which is shaken over and over again in a winnowing-basket, and which under its own weight always falls more and more purified of the light chaff which was debasing it.

There are the gentle passions which are always necessary, and which are developed all the more as humanity is perfected; and there are the others, violent and terrible, such as hatred and vengeance, which are developed more in times of barbarism; they are also natural, and thus also necessary. Their explosion brings back the gentle passions to ameliorate them. In the same way, violent fermentation is indispensable in the making of good wine.

Men who are taught by experience become more and more humane; and it would appear that in recent times generosity, the virtues, and the tender affections, which are continually spreading, at any rate in Europe, are diminishing the dominion of vengeance and national hatreds. But before laws had formed manners, these odious passions were still necessary for the defence of individuals and peoples. They were, so to speak, the leading-strings with which nature and its Author guided the human race in its infancy.

Man is still barbarous in America; and in early times in the rest of the world he was almost always cruel to foreigners. This blind partiality towards his own country, which lasted until Christianity and afterwards philosophy taught him to love all men, resembles the state of those animals which during the winter are covered with thick and hideous coats of fur which they will shed in the spring; or, if you like, his early passions resemble the first leaves which sheathe and hide the new stem of a plant, later withering with the emergence of other sheaths until as a result of these successive growths the stem is revealed and becomes crowned with flowers and fruits. This theory is not at all derogatory of Providence. The crimes which were committed were the crimes of men. Those who indulged in them were not happy; for no happiness can lie in the guilty passions. Those who drew on courage and virtue to resist them had their first reward in the consciousness of this courageous virtue. The struggle of one against the other increased the knowledge and the talents of all, and gave to the perception of the good a character of certainty which from day to day appeals more strongly to man's conscience, and a charm which will end by governing the hearts of all. If we look at the world from a broad point of view, then, and see it in the context of the whole concatenation of events which has characterised its progress, it becomes the most glorious witness to the wisdom which presides over it.

It is only through upheavals and ravages that nations have been extended, and that order and government have in the long run been perfected; just as in those forests of America, as old as the world, where from century to century oaks have succeeded to oaks, where from century to century, falling into the dust, they have enriched the soil with all the fruitful juices which the air and the rain have helped to provide, where their remains, furnishing a new source of fecundity to the earth which had given them birth, have served to produce new shoots, still hardier and more vigorous. Thus, over the whole surface of the earth governments have succeeded to governments, empires have been raised up on the ruins of empires, and their scattered remains have been gathered together again; the progress of reason under the early governments, freed from the constraint of the imperfect laws imposed by absolute power, has played a greater part in the constitution of later governments. Repeated conquests extended states; the impotence of barbarian laws and the limitations of civil authority forced them to divide. In some places, peoples weary of anarchy threw themselves into the arms of despotism; in others, tyranny carried to excess gave rise to liberty. No change took place without bringing about some gain; for none took place without adding to experience, and without extending or improving, or paving the way for, man's education. It was only after centuries, and by means of bloody revolutions, that despotism at last learned to moderate itself, and liberty to regulate itself; that the situation of states at last became less fluctuating and more stable. In this way, then, through alternate periods of rest and unrest, of weal and woe, the human race as a whole has advanced ceaselessly towards its perfection.

When quarrels first took place in nations, a man who was superior in strength, in valour, or in prudence persuaded and then forced the very people whom he was defending to obey him.

This superiority alone suffices to give a chief to men who have gathered together. It is not exactly true that ambition is the sole source of authority. People are induced to choose a chief; but they have always wished him to be reasonable and just, not foolish and arbitrary.

In nations of a small size it is impossible for despotic authority to become consolidated; the dominion of a chief can in such a nation rest on nothing but the consent of the people, or on a veneration either for a person or for a family. Veneration for a person disappears when power is abused; and when the veneration is for a family, this abuse provides a motive for palace revolutions for the benefit of another member of the family who seeks to gratify public opinion to a greater extent.

In small nations, the whole state is under the eyes of each individual. Each shares directly in the advantages of the society, and could not find any greater benefit in oppressing it on account of another. There is not enough wealth which could be used arbitrarily to bribe dishonest people. There is no populace: a kind of equality prevails. The kings could not live in isolation from their subjects; their people necessarily constitute their only guards and their only court. They love them better, and, when they are wise, they are better loved by them. If they are not wise, protests are soon made to them, and these could be followed by resistance. It is easy to assemble together. The means and the art of forcing the greater number, in spite of their size, to obey the smaller number cannot exist. Five hundred thousand men can keep in subjection fifty million, but two hundred men can never keep in subjection twenty thousand, although this is the same proportion. This explains why despotism has never held sway among peoples who are separated into small nations, Savages, Tartars, Celts, Arabs, etc., at any rate when some superstitious belief has not blinded men's eyes, as in the case of the subjects of the Old Man of the Mountain. This also explains why monarchy itself, which was everywhere the first form of government – since it is easier to control men than to get them to agree, and because military authority, always concentrated as it is in one hand, must have rendered a similar concentration of civil power natural and often necessary – was after a certain period replaced by republics in almost all those cities which were reduced to their adjoining territories or to distant colonies. Here the spirit of equality cannot be banished, because the spirit of commerce rules: the collective industry of men never fails to make it dominate in cities, when their ways of life are not corrupted and swallowed up by the general impulsive force of a huge state which encompasses them all: whether by the spirit of despotism, as in the case of the Asiatics; or whether, as in the case of the ancient Franks, by the military spirit of a nobility which resided in the countryside, and which had derived its original modes of behaviour in nomadic nations which could have no commerce. Also the spirit of commerce presupposes a property in goods which is independent of every power other than that of the laws: it cannot become inured to oriental *avania*.

In states which were confined to a single city, it was impossible that the monarchy could be long maintained. There its least transgressions are and are seen to be more tyrannical; there tyranny has less power and faces more energetic resistance. There, too, monarchy more easily degenerates. The passions of the man are more confounded with those of the prince. He or those in his circle may be tempted by some individual's fortune, or by his wife. Less elevated above his subjects, he is more sensitive to their affronts, and more susceptible to anger. In the infancy of human reason, it is easy for a prince to grow angry at the obstacles which the laws put in the way of his passions, and for him not to appreciate that these barriers between him and his people do not defend him less against his subjects than they do his subjects against him. But since in a small state he is never the strongest, the abuse of power, which is bound to be more frequent there, is also less easily defended against the revolt which is its consequence. Thus republics arise, at first aristocratic and more tyrannical than monarchy, because nothing is so horrible as obedience to a multitude which always knows how to exalt its passions into virtues; but at the same time more lasting, because the people are more debased. The powerful and the weak unite against a tyrant; but an aristocratic senate, above all if it is hereditary, has only the populace to combat. In spite of this,

73

republics confined to one city tend naturally towards democracy, which also has its serious drawbacks.

The domain of a city could be extended only by colonies and conquests. Colonies could be established in the vicinity of a city only in the earliest times. Soon the territory which surrounded the city became occupied; colonies were then removed to a distance, and consequently remained linked to the metropolis only in so far as they were not firmly enough established to be able to do without it, like those layers which remain attached to the trunk until they have grown strong enough, and which are then detached from it by the slightest accident; or like the fruit which clings to the tree until its maturity causes it to fall to the ground, germinate, and produce new trees. Nevertheless, by the use of a metaphor which was natural enough, the relations between the metropolis and the colonies were expressed by the words *mother* and *daughter*; men, who at all times have been bound by their own language, inferred analogous duties from these expressions, and the exercise of these duties was for a long time maintained solely by the force of custom, which always finds defenders among the men whom it subjugates, just as laws do among the authorities who maintain them.

It is rare for cities to make conquests. They go in for them only when, so to speak, they have nothing better to do. Moreover, there is commonly found among them a kind of equilibrium and a degree of jealousy sufficient to result in the formation of leagues against any city which exalts itself too much.

Love of country, above all in republics, makes it almost impossible for the sovereignty of a city to be destroyed by forces which are the equal of its own.

Thus a city is rarely a conqueror, barring some unusual combination of internal constitution and external circumstances which was never found, I believe, except in the case of the Roman people.

But when cities were still under the sway of kings, it was easier to make conquests. A warlike king gave a considerable superiority to his city; he could make a number of conquests and bring several cities under his domination; and the more his city was extended the stronger became his authority, and the more possible it became for him to crush one party through the instrumentality of the others. The authority of the prince became the sole centre of power, and whatever interest individuals might have or appear to have in throwing off the yoke, it was impossible for them to be brought together except through a long series of secret intrigues; but the king was usually powerful enough for fear or hope of reward to induce some accomplice to betray such a secret.

Unreasoning ambition often drove the first conquerors to spread out far and wide, and when it proved impossible, either for want of troops or because the distances were too great, to maintain their conquests, they contented themselves with exacting tribute, which was only paid so long as the people concerned were weaker.

Hence a perpetual succession of wars, and a continual alternation of victories and defeats, of nations in turn dominating one another, according as chance gave them kings who were conquerors.

In the case of those princes ruling over agricultural peoples who were up to a point civilised, their states were bound, because of the inequality in the progress of their neighbours, to find themselves surrounded by barbarous peoples. When they were in their vigorous stage, they extended their power by making conquests, by turning the neighbouring territories into colonies and gradually civilising them. But when such states relapsed into weakness, the barbarians attacked them in their turn and had the best of it; the desire to dominate a rich country pricked the ambition of the chiefs and the greed of a fierce people.

These inundations, these migrations of peoples which among barbarians succeed one another without leaving any trace, sometimes encompassed in their course peoples who were already civilised, and it is only in this way that the memory of them has been able to come down to us today. In such cases the barbarian people adopted the civilisation of the conquered, as a result of the influence which knowledge and reason are always certain to exercise over force when conquest does not involve extermination. The barbarians, having become civilised, themselves civilised their first place of abode. The two peoples were formed into a single people; it became a more extensive empire under one chief.

Civilised peoples, who are more wealthy, more peaceful, and more accustomed to a soft or at any rate sedentary life, above all in the fertile regions which were the first to be cultivated, soon lose that vigour which made them into conquerors when a learned discipline puts no obstacle at all in the way of softness. The conquerors then give way to new barbarians; empires are extended, going through their ages of vigour and decline; but their very downfall helps to perfect the arts and improve the laws. Thus the Chaldeans, the Assyrians, the Medes, and the Persians succeeded one another, the domination of the latter being the most far-reaching.

It was in this way that the kingdom of Lydia, when it had acquired a degree of superiority, swallowed up all the little kingdoms of Asia Minor, which had been softened by the Greek way of life. Later, like those rivers which, swollen by the contributions of a thousand others, eventually lose themselves in the sea, Lydia was in its turn invaded by Cyrus, who appeared with a new nation. This nation, at first barbarous, retained under the conqueror's successors nothing but pride and ambition. The softness of the vanquished was soon transmitted to the victors. That discipline which alone can offset force, and by means of which the reason of enlightened peoples makes up for the violence of barbarians, was known only by the Greeks. The whole of the great Persian power broke down against Greece, which had taken shape and developed in the midst of civil wars.

The territory of Greece, broken up by islands and mountains, could not be subject to the same vicissitudes. It was difficult in early times for great empires to be formed there. A host of small states, almost always at war, kept up the military spirit, and made advances in tactical skills, the perfection of arms, and boldness in battle. Civilisation was also extended by means of commerce. In general it is peoples from the mountains and from cold or infertile countries who have conquered the plains, and who have either formed empires or held out against them. They are poorer, more hardy, and more inaccessible; they can choose their time when they are attacking and their positions when they are defending themselves. And when they are desirous of becoming conquerors, they have more to gain from it, and a greater aptitude for it.

The great empires, formed as we have just said by barbarians, were despotic. Despotism is easy. To do what you want to do, is a rule which a king learns very quickly; art is necessary to persuade people, but none is necessary to give them orders. If despotism did not revolt those who are its victims, it would never be banished from the earth. A father wishes to be a despot over his children, and a master over his servants. Honesty does not safeguard a prince against this poison; he wishes for the good, and makes a virtue of wishing everyone to obey him. The larger the state the easier despotism is, and the greater would be the difficulty involved in establishing a moderate government. For that, it would be necessary for there to be an established order in all parts of the state; one would have to determine the position of each province and of each city, and to allow its municipal administration all the liberty which it would not be possible for it to abuse. How many different departments would have to be combined and equilibrated, and what difficulties would face him who had no idea that this was necessary! A conquest carried out by barbarians, which is the product of force and accompanied by devastation, puts a state into such disorder that to mend matters would require the greatest genius, the most dexterous hand, the most moderate and active virtue, and the purest and noblest heart.

Since it was impossible to answer for everything, one could devise nothing better than to install governors who were as despotic to the people as they were servile to the prince. It was easier to look to them to levy taxes and keep the people down than to arrange the details of this oneself.

The prince forgot the people. The best governor was the one who gave him the most money and who knew best how to obtain the menials and flatterers who frequented the palace. The governors had underlings who acted in the same way. Despotic authority made the governors dangerous; the court treated them with the utmost severity, and their position depended upon its slightest caprice. Pretexts were sought to deprive them of the treasure they had plundered; and the people gained no relief at all, for greed is a natural characteristic of barbarian kings.

Originally taxes were never conceived as subventions to meet the needs of the state; but the prince demanded money, and people were forced to give it to him. Throughout the east presents are made to them; the kings there are simply individuals who are powerful and greedy.

All power was thus concentrated in a single person, who was not even shrewd enough to divide up that part of it which he was unable to exercise. Princes, governors, and underlings were alike subordinate tyrants who exerted pressure on one another only in order to crush the people with all their united strength.

Despotic princes, never having come across laws, scarcely dreamed of making any. They were their own judges: in general, when the power which makes the laws and that which applies them are one and the same, the laws are useless. Punishments remain arbitrary; they are usually cruel when they are imposed by the prince, and pecuniary in character when they are imposed by underlings who draw profit from them. So far as the civil disposition of inheritances is concerned, custom or the will of the father decides it.

It can also be seen from this that a despotic government which comes on the scene after laws and customs have been established does not involve the same disadvantages as these early conquests made by barbarians did.

The Neros and the Caligulas, if I may venture to say so, had in them more wickedness than the evil they actually committed. As a result of the rules of conduct accepted in the state under the first Caesars, the people were not at all oppressed; the provinces enjoyed a high degree of tranquillity; and distributive justice was equitably enough carried out. The governors did not dare to give way to their greed: they would have been punished by the emperors. The court held, between the people and the great, that balance which it ought to hold in a well-directed government.

In general, the most moderate of the great states are those which are formed by the union of several small ones, above all when this union is brought about slowly.

At bottom, the monarch has no interest at all in involving himself with the details of municipal government in places where he is never present: he is led to leave it as it is. Princes can be partial to despotism only when it is around them, because their passions (or those at least which are most subject to caprice) are relative only to what is in their neighbourhood: like the rest, they are not more than human. That is why the despotism of the Roman emperors did less harm than that of the Turks.

With the Turks, despotism enters into the constitution of their government. It infects all parts of the state; it fetters all its departments. Each pasha exercises over the people who are subject to him the same authority which the Grand Seigneur has over him. He is alone entrusted with and responsible for all the tribute. He has no other revenue than that which he extracts from the people over and above what he is obliged to furnish to the sultan; and he is forced to redouble his harassments in order to provide for the countless presents which are necessary to keep him in his office. There is no law in the empire to regulate the raising of money, and no formal procedure in the administration of justice. Everything is done in military fashion. The people have no one at all at court to protect them against the abuse of power by the great, in the fruits of which the court itself shares.

When it is the conqueror who has himself installed governors in the provinces, his ignorance is bound to lead him to take his own government as a model, and thus to establish an administrative despotism, which then becomes as it were a great tree whose branches spread out far and wide over the whole empire, and which smother all the produce of the land which they cover with their shadow.

When a military government is the only thing which keeps the state together, forming a nation only by making it the slave of a prince, this government is despotic in principle, and if manners do not moderate it, it will also be so in practice. Military discipline necessarily presupposes despotism and rigour. But we must not confuse nations ruled by a military government with nations wholly composed of warriors, such as the barbarians, Germans and others. Far from it: their government gives birth to liberty. There war is by no means an exclusive occupation which has to be specially studied, and which gives those who carry it on a superiority of force over the rest of society. Such a nation maintains its rights. A prince can enslave his people by means of soldiers, because the people are weaker. But how can he enslave a people of soldiers? It is not courage, nor the military spirit, which extinguish liberty, but the very reverse.

The kingdoms of Europe conquered by the northern barbarians, therefore, were saved from despotism, because these barbarians were free before the conquest, which was carried out in the name of the people and not in that of the king. The Roman way of life which was established, and the religion which the barbarians embraced, also contributed to protect them from despotism.

Private individuals were spread throughout the country; they shared territorial power and the gains of victory with the prince.

It was not the same in Asia, where the conquered peoples were already accustomed to despotism, because the first conquests, which had taken place before the period when manners could have been formed, had been very extensive and rapid.

Despotism gives birth to revolutions; but all that these bring about is the exchange of one tyrant for another, because in great despotic states the power of the kings is established only by means of their troops, and their security by means of their guards. The people are never strong or united enough to check such a military power, which substitutes one king for another, assured of being the instrument of the tyranny of the successor as it had been of that of his predecessor.

One suspects that the total effects of these causes must have been infinitely various, depending upon the way in which they were intermixed with the ideas of the received religion, and, as we have already noted, with veneration for a particular family, because in the absence of any other power men are ruled by habit. It would have been just as easy for the janissaries, if they had wanted to, to choose a sultan from among the populace as from the Ottoman family; but such was the respect for that family which was instilled into them from infancy that they would not have wanted this.

This power of education is one of the main sources of the capacity of governments to endure, to the point of maintaining them when the whole driving force of the empire is weakened, and of concealing its decline: in such a way that at the slightest disturbance one is astonished to see the state fall to the ground, like those trees which look healthy, because their bark is undamaged, whereas all the wood inside it is reduced to powder,

79

and no longer offers any resistance to the wind. In despotic states, education is wholly employed to break down people's courage. Fear and deference seize hold of the imagination. The sovereign, wrapped in formidable obscurity, seems to govern from the depths of a storm cloud, from which come thunder and lightning to inspire terror and dazzle.

It may be added that in these vast despotic states there is also introduced a despotism which extends over social manners, which dulls men's minds even more; which deprives society of the greater part of its resources, its delights, and the co-operation of women in the running of the family; which by forbidding the social intercourse of the two sexes reduces everything to uniformity, and induces in members of the state a tired lethargy which is opposed to all change and therefore to all progress.

When everything is conducted by force (as it necessarily has to be in a society where a host of slaves and women – in each wealthy house as in the state itself – are sacrificed to a single master), the fire of the intellect is extinguished; it is locked in the shackles of barbarian laws. Despotism perpetuates ignorance, and ignorance perpetuates despotism. What is more, this despotic authority becomes common practice, and common practice confirms the abuses. Despotism is like an enormous weight which, pressing down on wooden pillars, weakens their resistance and causes them from day to day to sink and subside.

I shall therefore say something about slavery, polygamy, and the softness which is their consequence; and under this head I shall deal with the causes of differences in manners among men.

The enslavement of women to men is based over the whole world on the inequality of their physical powers. But as rather more men are born than women, wherever equality has reigned monogamy has been natural. It is so, therefore, among all small peoples, shepherds, hunters, and husbandmen; it is so among peoples divided up into small societies where the states are confined within the walls of cities as in Greece, and above all in the democratic republics; it is so among poor peoples, and among all the less wealthy individuals in the very countries where polygamy is most in vogue; it is the same in the empires whose customs date from the time when the people were still under republican governments, like the Roman empire and that of Alexander's successors, which although despotic never knew polygamy.

Nevertheless the barbarians, who show little refinement in matters of love, were all inclined towards plurality of wives. Tacitus reports that the chiefs of the Germans sometimes had three or four wives; but among a people which was nomadic and poor the evil could not have been contagious. Thus it was with the growth in the wealth and the size of empires that polygamy was established; and with slavery its extent was increased.

The first men were cruel in their wars; it was only after a long time that they learned moderation. Hunting peoples massacre their prisoners; or, when they do not kill them, they incorporate them in their own nation. A mother who has lost her son chooses a prisoner to serve as a son to her; she loves him because he is useful to her. The ancients, among whom children were a form of wealth, and who received services from them, were inclined towards the adoption of children. Thus there were few slaves, or none at all, among hunting or primitive peoples.

Pastoral peoples began to be familiar with slavery. Those who captured herds were obliged, in order to be able to devote themselves to new expeditions, to maintain those who tended them.

Agricultural peoples carried slavery further. They had more varied services and more tiring work for slaves to perform, and in proportion to the extent to which the manners of the masters became more civilised, slavery became harsher and more degrading, because the inequality was greater. The wealthy ceased to work; slaves became a luxury and a commodity; parents even sold their children. But the slaves who were captured in war, or who were born of parents who were themselves slaves, always made up the greatest number.

In the house, they were used for all the lowest duties. They had neither goods nor honour of their own; they were stripped of the elementary rights of humanity. The laws gave limitless authority over them, and this was quite easy, because it was their masters who made the laws; and these masters thought to assure oppression by means of oppression. In despotic states the princes had a host of slaves, as did the governors and even wealthy individuals. The vast size of the states brought the inequality of fortunes to the highest pitch. The capitals became like chasms, where the wealthy from all parts of the empire gathered together, along with their hosts of slaves.

The female slaves formed part of the master's pleasures. This can be seen in the manners of the ancient patriarchs, for the crime of adultery (and this was still the case in the statute law of antiquity) was never a reciprocal one as it is with us. It was only the husband who was regarded as being injured by it. This was a consequence of the great inequality between the two sexes which barbarism brought about. Among the ancient peoples women never had any rights in the marriage relation. It was only poverty which prevented polygamy from being established everywhere.

When in later times the manners and laws of a nation became settled, the intermingling of families restored to women those *rights* which they had not enjoyed since the earliest times, because, above all in republics, they used the power of their brothers against the tyranny of their husbands.

In these republics, where everyone was equal, the parents of a girl would never have agreed to let her go out of their sight for ever. Polygamy and the cloistering of women could never become established there. But in the first empires of which we are speaking, peopled as they were by a host of slaves, where women had no rights, and men had rights over their slaves, the plurality of wives became a practice which was as common as the limits of individual fortunes allowed. Jealousy is a necessary consequence of love: it inspires husband and wife with a wise sense of mutual propriety which assures the future of their children. This sensible attitude, and still more the presumption of dishonour which was associated with a wife's infidelity, increased along with polygamy.

The impossibility of subjecting women to this law of fidelity, when neither their hearts nor their senses could be satisfied, led to the practice of shutting them up. Princes, and later those individuals who were wealthy enough, established seraglios for themselves.

Jealousy brought it about that men were mutilated in order to guard the women. Thence a softness entered into manners which did not mollify them but on the contrary rendered them more cruel.

The princes shut themselves up with their wives and their slaves; and their subjects, whom they never saw, were scarcely regarded by them as human beings. Their political government was always that of barbarians. It was crude, because they were ignorant and lazy; it was cruel, because less time is required to cut down a tree than to gather in its fruits, and because the art of making men happy is of all arts the most difficult, the one in which the most elements have to be combined.

The same softness spread through the whole state. Thence that sudden weakening of the monarchies of the east. Those of the Chaldeans, the Assyrians, the Medes, and the Persians scarcely survived the first conquerors who had founded them. It was as if they had remained in being for some time only while waiting for an enemy to come and destroy them. If these monarchies, by the weight of their armies, sometimes overwhelmed weak nations, they broke down in the face of any courageous resistance; and as soon as Greece had been united, it overthrew this immense colossus with hardly any effort.

There is only one means available to counter this general degeneracy of a nation, and that is a militia which is kept under martial discipline, like the Turkish janissaries or the Egyptian mamelukes; but such a militia often becomes an object of terror to its masters.

One thing that should be pointed out is that these harmful effects of despotism and the plurality of wives have never been extended so far as under Mohammedanism. This religion, which does not allow any laws other than those of the religion itself, opposes the wall of superstition to the natural march of improvement. It has consolidated barbarism by *consecrating* that which existed when it appeared, and which it adopted through national prejudice. Neither in the history of the ancient monarchies, nor in the manners of China and Japan, can one find such an excess of abasement as that of the Mohammedan peoples.

Despotism, and the uniformity and thus the imperfection of manners, laws, and government, were maintained in Asia and wherever great empires were formed at an early stage; and I have no doubt that the existence of the vast plains of Mesopotamia contributed to this. When despotism was later extended along with Mohammedanism, this was to some extent only as a result of the transmission of manners from one country to another.

The peoples who were preserved from despotism were those who remained shepherds or hunters; those who formed small societies; and the republics. It was among such peoples that revolutions were useful; that nations participated in them and thus drew gain from them; that tyranny was unable to consolidate itself sufficiently to enslave men's minds; that the profusion of particular bodies of law and of revolutions which pointed out the errors of the founders of the state, and the fall of an old and rise of a new sovereign authority which brought about a re-examination of the laws, in the long run perfected the laws and government. It was among such peoples that equality was maintained, that intellect and courage showed great activity, and that the human mind made rapid progress. It was among them that manners and laws in the course of time learned how to direct themselves towards the greatest happiness of the people.

After this glance at the progress of governments and their morality, it will be useful to trace the progress of the human mind in all its revolutions.

SKETCH OF THE SECOND DISCOURSE

Of which the subject will be the Progress of the Human Mind

Let us start from that state of confusion in which the mind knows nothing but sensations, in which sounds, more or less loud and more or less shrill, the temperature and resistance of surrounding objects, and pictures of bizarre, differently coloured forms, come to assail the mind on every hand, and throw it into a kind of intoxication which is nevertheless the germ of reason.

The manner in which ideas begin to become a little distinct in our minds, and to exercise an influence on our will, depends on a kind of spiritual mechanism common to all men. It may be the work of a few moments; at any rate this would seem to be proved by the example of animals which know how to find their food, and, what would appear more difficult, which know how to go and look for it shortly after their birth.

Although pertaining to the history of nature rather than to that of facts, this period must be studied with care, since in every sphere the first steps determine the direction of the journey.

It was movement which cleared up this state of confusion, and which gave men the ideas of distinction and unity. Without it, they would never have thought of reflecting on the difference between colours; they would have been content merely to experience it. But the arrangement of the parts of this picture which is presented to the mind often changes the picture itself. The mind learns to observe the course of these variations. During the first experience of these changes, no distinction at all was yet made between the parts which maintained the same position relative to one another, whether the whole appeared to be in motion, as in the case of animals, or whether it appeared to be fixed in one spot, as in that of a tree. Thus, however much the images presented to our senses were only the result of all the individual coloured or resistant points of which they were composed, the mind conceived them, so to speak, only in bulk.

The first individual ideas were thus necessarily collective in relation to the parts of which they are composed; at no time was it possible, nor will it ever be possible, for the analysis of the works of men to be carried to the highest degree. Properly speaking, there are no such things as simple ideas; they all resolve themselves into the results of sensations, the elements and different causes of which can be analysed up to a point whose limit is unknown to us.

But the analysis of the first men was not carried very far. The stock of ideas was divided up only to the extent of the experience afforded by the diversity of phenomena and above all of needs. Men's needs are relative only to this stock; it is unnecessary to anatomise fruits in order to feed on them, and even less necessary to analyse the ideas which inform us of their presence. Ideas are a language and true indicators by means of which we recognise the existence of external objects. It is never by means of reasoning that we perceive their relations with ourselves. Providence, by inspiring us with desires, has wisely spared us so long a journey. As a result of this, men have necessarily related their sensations to the external objects which they assume to exist. Where would we be if, before going in search of their food, men had been obliged, from their own sensations regarded solely as affections of their minds, to infer the existence of objects outside themselves?

Thus men began by giving names which were relative to the existing stock of ideas. Ideas, being the indicators of the existence of external objects, do not represent them at all exactly; from a distance an oak looks like an elm, and thus arises the idea of *a tree* – not because I have the idea of a tree which is neither an oak nor an elm, but because I have an idea which informs me of the existence of a tree without telling me whether it is the one or the other. This is the origin of abstraction. The idea is simple, no doubt, if one considers it in itself, independent of its relations – i.e., if we take it as always representing a certain form and a certain colour; but experience teaches us that this form and this colour are equally an indicator of the existence of an oak or of an elm.

It is the same with the signs of language. The first time they were used they designated only some definite object; but as they were applied to several objects they became general. Little by little different circumstances were distinguished, and in order to import more clarity into language, names were given to *modes* or *manners of being*, which in relation to our ideas are only relations of distance, or rather relations to the different sensations which are excited in us by the different languages which the objects speak to us, if I may put it that way.

Thus the ideas of *modes* were given names after those of *substances*, which were regarded as the principal ideas, although the senses acquire them for us at one and the same time. Thus it was by extracting the signs of language from their undue generality that the mind familiarised itself little by little with more abstract ideas. One suspects that ideas were multiplied in proportion as languages were perfected. The words which expressed affirmation, negation, the act of judging, existence, and possession became the bond of all our reasoning. Habit caused these same ideas to be applied in similar cases to all the roots of languages.

Little by little, by giving names in this way to the different relations which objects have with one another or with ourselves, the possession of all these ideas was assured, and as a result the operations of the mind acquired a considerable facility. But at the same time the labyrinth of ideas became more and more encumbered; it was natural to believe that to each word there corresponded one idea, and yet the same words are rarely synonymous with one another; they have different meanings according to the way in which they are applied. In conversation we guess more than we actually hear.

The mind, by an almost mechanical operation which owes its origin to the linking together of ideas, seizes quite quickly the meaning of words determined by the circumstances. Having believed that words corresponded exactly to ideas, men were quite astonished to see that their precise determination could not be agreed upon; it was a long time before they began to suspect that this arose from the fact that ideas were different according as one wanted to extract the general idea from different particular cases; people lost their way among misleading definitions which took in only one part of the object, and everyone gave a different definition of the same idea.

The complex notions of substance, which, because they relate to real objects, necessarily include a greater or lesser number of parts, according as the object is more or less understood, were regarded as pictures of the objects themselves. Instead of asking by what stages a certain number of different kinds of things had been gathered together under a general name, an effect of which the cause would have been found in their general resemblance, men sought for that common essence which the names expressed; they invented genera, species, individuals, and those *metaphysical degrees* whose nature has caused so many disputes, as cruel sometimes in their effects as they were frivolous in their object.

Instead of regarding these names as signs which are relative to the manner in which we perceive the range of existing things which we extend according to the resemblances we discover, and which we cannot extend too far without running the risk of confusing one with another, men invented *abstract and incommunicable essences*. Latterly they have gone so far as to apply this also to concepts relating to products of the human mind, such as comedy and tragedy. People have seriously argued about whether a poem belongs to this or that genus, and only rarely has it been realised that the argument is merely about words.

The error was still greater with regard to the signs which were used
to express the relations between things. Such are all the moral ideas
which have been reasoned about as if they were objects existing independently of the things which have these relations with one another.

Man receives his various ideas in his infancy, or, rather, the words are
engraved on his mind. They are linked up at first with particular ideas;
and little by little there is formed that confused assemblage of ideas and
expressions whose use is learned through imitation. Time, by means of
the progress of languages, has multiplied ideas to infinity; and when man
seeks to retire within himself, he finds himself in a labyrinth which he
has entered with blindfolded eyes. He can no longer find the marks of
his footsteps; nevertheless his eyes open, and he sees on all sides paths of
whose interconnection he is unaware. He clings to a few truths which he
is unable to doubt; but whence does this certainty come to him? He
knows nothing except through his ideas, and he is thus bound to believe
that his ideas bring certainty with them; for whence could he derive it
before having analysed the manner in which these ideas are formed in
his mind? This is an immense task, which requires several generations.

Without understanding very well what it is to have an idea of a thing,
he lays down as a principle that everything which his ideas tell him about
an object is true. This is a delusive principle, because in reality it is an art
to draw from notions once they have been determined, even arbitrarily,
inferences which are incapable of taking one in. Success, in this case,
becomes another source of error. People have more confidence in the
principle, and misuse of it does not arouse any aversion to it at all. For
the same reason that everyone is convinced that he has the true idea of an
object, one is never tempted to challenge a court, to which no one has
recourse without believing that he will hear it pronounce in his favour.
From this in all ages there has arisen the obscurity of logic and metaphysics; from this have arisen arbitrary definitions and divisions.

This darkness could only be dissipated little by little; the dawn of
reason could only rise by imperceptible degrees, to the extent that men
analysed their ideas more and more; not that they at first recognised the
necessity of distinguishing between all the parts of their ideas: but their
very disputes led them towards this, because truth seems to fly away and
escape from our investigations until we have arrived at the primary
elements of ideas; because while advancing little by little we are always
aware of a gap; and finally because curiosity always makes us act until
it has exhausted the subject of its investigations, and because no question
can be exhausted except by means of the truth.

Progress was more or less rapid, depending on circumstances and aptitudes.

A fortunate arrangement of the fibres of the brain, a greater or lesser degree of power or refinement in the organs of sense and memory, a certain degree of quickness in the blood – these are probably the only differences which nature herself creates as between one man and another. Their minds, or the power and character of their minds, have a real inequality, the causes of which will always remain unknown to us and which could never be the subject of our reasoning. All the rest is the effect of education; and this education is the result of all the sensations we have experienced, and of all the ideas which we have been able to acquire from infancy. All the objects with which we are surrounded contribute to this; and the instruction of our parents and our masters makes up only the smallest part of it.

The original aptitudes are distributed equally among barbarous peoples and among civilised peoples; they are probably the same in all places and at all times. Genius is spread through the human race very much as gold is in a mine. The more ore you take, the more metal you will get. The more men there are, the more great men you will have, or the more men capable of becoming great. The chances of education and of events either develop them, or leave them buried in obscurity, or sacrifice them before their time, like fruits blown down by the wind. One is compelled to admit that if Corneille, brought up in a village, had followed the plough all his life, that if Racine had been born in Canada among the Hurons, or in Europe in the eleventh century, they would never have unfolded their genius. If Columbus and Newton had died at sixteen, America would perhaps not have been discovered until two centuries later, and we would still perhaps be ignorant of the true system of the world. And if Virgil had perished in infancy we would have had no Virgil, for there have not been two of them.

Progress, although inevitable, is intermingled with frequent periods of decline as a result of the occurrences and revolutions which come to interrupt it. Thus progress has been very different among different peoples.

Men who are separated from one another and who have no commerce have moved forward at much the same rate. We have found small nations which live by hunting at the same point of development, with the same arts, the same arms, and the same manners. Genius was of little benefit with respect to unrefined needs; but as soon as the human race succeeded in escaping from the narrow sphere of these elementary needs, the circumstances which put this genius in a position to develop, combined with those which presented it with facts and experiences which a thousand others would have seen without taking advantage of them, soon introduced one or another kind of inequality.

Among barbarous peoples, where education is more or less the same for everyone, this inequality could not be very great. When labour was divided according to men's aptitudes, which is in itself very advantageous since everything is then done better and more quickly, the unequal distribution of goods and social responsibilities meant that the majority of men who were employed in rough and lowly work were unable to make the same progress as the other men, to whom this distribution gave leisure and the means of advancing themselves.

Education brought about an even greater difference between the various parts of one and the same nation than did wealth, and as between different nations it was the same.

The people which was the first to acquire a little more knowledge quickly became superior to its neighbours; and each step in its progress made the next one easier. Thus the development of one nation accelerated from day to day, while others stayed in their state of mediocrity, immobilised by particular circumstances, and others remained in a state of barbarism. A glance over the earth puts before our eyes, even today, the whole history of the human race, showing us traces of all the steps and monuments of all the stages through which it has passed from the barbarism, still in existence, of the American peoples to the civilisation of the most enlightened nations of Europe. Alas! our ancestors and the Pelasgians who preceded the Greeks were like the savages of America!

A reason for these differences which are found between nations has been sought in differences of climate. This view, modified a little and rightly restricted only to those climatic influences which are always the same, has recently been adopted by one of the greatest geniuses of our century. But the conclusions which are drawn from it are hasty, to say the least, and are extremely exaggerated. They are belied by experience, since under the same climates peoples are different; since under climates which resemble one another very little we very often find peoples with the same character and the same turn of mind; since the fervour and despotism of the Orientals can arise from barbarism alone when it is combined with certain circumstances; and since that metaphorical language which is presented to us as an effect of the greater proximity of the sun was that of the ancient Gauls and Germans, according to the accounts given by Tacitus and Diodorus Siculus, and is still that of the

Iroquois in the icy regions of Canada. It is in fact that of all peoples whose language is very limited, and who, lacking the appropriate words, multiply comparisons, metaphors, and allusions in order to make themselves understood, and who manage this sometimes forcefully but always with little exactitude and clarity.

Since physical causes act only upon the hidden principles which contribute to the formation of our mind and our character, and not upon the results, which are all that we see, we are right to evaluate their influence only after having exhaustively examined that of the moral causes and assured ourselves that the facts are absolutely inexplicable by the latter, of whose principle we are conscious, and whose operation we can follow in the depths of our hearts.

The ideas of the first men were limited to objects perceptible by the senses, and thus their languages were confined to designating them. The formation of a host of abstract and general ideas, still unknown to a large number of peoples, was the work of time, and consequently it was only after a long period that men arrived at an understanding of the art of reasoning.

The class of objects which were the first to be designated in languages was the same everywhere, just as were the first metaphors and the first abstract ideas which govern conjugations, declensions, and analogy in the most barbarous languages (none of which we know in its original state); for whatever the way in which barbarism arrests the progress of a body of men, it is only by depriving them of opportunities to perfect themselves. In the course of time genius never fails to appear. Thus in the constant use of languages it is impossible that the variety of combinations of ideas which present themselves for expression should not indicate the need for new signs, in order to denote new connections or new shades of meaning between the ideas. And this need, which is a consciousness of our poverty, in revealing the latter to us teaches us how to remedy it, and becomes the source of our wealth.

Thus the languages of the most barbarous peoples are today very far removed from their first attempts. It is the same with all progress, which is always real but sometimes very slow; there are few arts and sciences whose origin cannot be traced back to these first epochs; all the arts are based on homely ideas, on experiences which are common to and within the reach of all men.

We see the immense progress which the sciences have made, and we have lost sight of the imperceptible chain by which they are linked to the first ideas. In the beginning, men observed the heavenly bodies with the naked eye; the horizon was the first instrument, and the 360 days of the lunisolar year are the model for the division of the circle into 360 degrees. The stars, from the first to the fourth magnitude, are visible to all men. The alternation of days and nights, and the changes in the phases of the moon, were natural measures of time; the alternation of heat and cold, and the needs of tillage, led to a comparison of the path of the sun with that of the moon. Thence the year, the months, and the names of the principal constellations.

Then navigation made it necessary to perfect astronomy, and showed how to relate it to geography.

Music, dance, and poetry, again, have their source in the nature of man. Created to live in society, his joy manifests itself externally: he leaps and shouts. A common joy expressed itself in swaying movements, in leaps, and in simultaneous and confused shouts. Little by little people became accustomed to leap in a similar manner; the steps were marked by sounds; and the latter were separated by regular intervals. The ear, with very little experience, and by following nature alone, learned to appreciate the primary relations between sounds. When it was desired to communicate the reason for one's joy in words, these were arranged according to the beat of the sounds. This was the origin of dance, of music, and of poetry, which was at first written in order to be sung. It was only with time that people began to get satisfaction simply from the harmony which was characteristic of it, and which they became familiar with only after it had been sufficiently perfected to give pleasure by itself alone. To the extent that the arts are perfected, they are separated from one another because they need particular talents. Pauses were indicated by similar sounds, and the ear thus learned to take account of the number of syllables. The necessity of conforming in this way to the beat must have contributed to the progress and softening of languages; versification daily became less free; the ear, by dint of experience, subjected itself to stricter rules; and if the burden of these became heavier, this was fortunately compensated for by the fact that the perfection of languages and the proliferation of new turns of phrase and felicitous boldnesses of style also lent greater strength to bear it.

Among uncultivated peoples, the capacity to remember verses, together with national vanity, induced them to set down in songs their most memorable actions. Such are the songs of the savages of our own day, those of the ancient bards, the runic rhymes of the inhabitants of Scandinavia, some ancient canticles included in the historical books of the Hebrews; the chou-king of the Chinese, and the ballads of the modern peoples of Europe. These were the only histories which existed before the invention of writing – histories without chronology, and, as we might expect, often full of untrue circumstances.

The poverty of languages, and the necessity for metaphors which resulted from this poverty, led to the employment of allegories and fables to explain physical phenomena. They are the first steps of philosophy, as can still be seen in India.

The fables of all peoples resemble one another, because the effects to be explained, and the patterns of the causes which have been invented in order to explain them, resemble one another. There are some differences, because although there is only one truth, and although imagination takes only one course which is very much the same everywhere, the individual steps do not all correspond with one another. Moreover, the mythological beings who were supposed to exist were brought into histories of the facts, which thus came to vary greatly. The sex of the gods, often depending as it did on the gender of a word in a language, was also bound to bring about variations in the fables of different peoples. Very many circumstances in these fables were peculiar to them, without destroying their general interrelationship. The intermingling of nations, and trade between them, gave birth to new fables through ambiguities of expression; and poorly understood words increased the number of the old fables.

Regarding imaginary beings as real, men sometimes multiplied the number of gods by including those which different nations had invented to explain the same effects, and at other times they took those which had similar attributes to be the same. Thence the confusion in the history of these gods. Thence too the multiplicity of their actions, above all when two peoples with the same mythologies were mixed together, as in the case of the Indians. Natural philosophy changed, but people did not stop believing in fables, because of their twofold love of antiquity and the marvellous, and also because the fables were transmitted from century to century by education.

The first histories were also fables, invented in the same way to make up for ignorance of the origin of empires, arts, and customs; it is very easy indeed to recognise their falsity. Everything which men invent is linked only to what seems to be the truth, that is, to the opinions of the century in which the fact concerned is invented. But what men recount is linked to the truth itself, and can never be contradicted by subsequent observations. Moreover, before the invention of writing, men had no records other than songs and a few stones beside which the songs were repeated. It is clear that men were more concerned to seek amusement and glory in these songs than they were to avoid exaggeration in them. Even Herodotus was still a poet. It was only after him that it was felt necessary that history should tell the truth.

Herodotus wrote four centuries after Homer, and yet what does Herodotus amount to? What then did those four centuries amount to? What were the times of Homer like? Why had poetry risen so high while history remained so low? Herodotus is vastly inferior in his field to Homer in his; and one of the great defects of Herodotus is that he is too like Homer, seeking all the time to decorate his account with the ornaments of fable. To know that men are greedy for the marvellous, to have enough genius to use it with vigour and grace, and to give general pleasure – that was Homer. More reflection was necessary, and a slower rate of progress, before it was understood that there were occasions when these marvels could not give as much pleasure as the unvarnished truth; that men's curiosity could find in the certainty of things a pleasure and a tranquillity which more than compensated for the number, variety, and singularity of the adventures; and finally that a means of giving pleasure which had been tried a thousand times could not be assured of success for ever.

This reflection and this progress were reserved for times after Homer's, and more than four centuries after. When Herodotus wrote, these times had not yet arrived. Often a thing which demands less genius than another requires more progress among mankind as a whole.

The arts of design, sculpture, and painting have many connections with poetry in the feelings which the artist experiences, and in those which he strives to communicate. They had a natural origin in the desire to preserve historical or mythological records; and genius in this sphere was heightened by that patriotic or religious zeal which sought to express with feeling, depth, and force the ideas and memories which these records were bound to recall.

All these arts depend a great deal on the different states of mankind – whether they are hunters, shepherds, or husbandmen. The latter, being the only ones who could have a large population, and needing as they did a greater amount of positive knowledge in order to direct their labour, would necessarily make much greater progress.

Men's knowledge, all of which is contained within actual sensation, is of different kinds. One kind consists in pure combinations of ideas, such as abstract mathematics. Another is concerned with external objects, but takes in, so to speak, only their surface and the effects they have on us:

such are poetry and the arts of taste. Another, finally, has for its object the very existence of things. It goes back from effects to causes, from the senses to the body, from the present to the past, from visible bodies to invisible ones, from the world to the Divinity. The belief in the existence of bodies, and that of past objects which are recalled by the memory, came before reasoning. No one ever had any doubts about the immediate cause of our sensations: the causes of the movements of bodies constituted physics; and at first the action of bodies upon one another was often confused with that of the Divinity.

Aristotle, in a work which, although scoffed at today, is none the less one of the finest endeavours of the human spirit, was able to carry analysis to its perfection by examining the manner in which our minds pass from a known truth to an unknown one; he was able to derive from this the rules of the art of reasoning, and by demonstrating the effects of a certain combination of ideas he showed how we could make certain that one proposition was legitimately deduced from another. It must be admitted that in the rest of his philosophy he was unable to make any analysis as perfect as this, because the enumeration of the ideas was not nearly as easy. But however useful one takes his work to be so far as consequences are concerned, it could not serve to ascertain causes. Although Aristotle had put forward the notion that all ideas came from the senses, it was a very long time before anyone began looking for causes other than the so-called abstract ideas and going back to their origin. *Bacon* was the first to feel the necessity for submitting all these notions to examination again. It was a great deal at that time to encourage scholars to do this. We must forgive him for having himself proceeded only in a timid fashion. He was like a man who walks trembling along a road filled with ruins, doubting and feeling his way. After him, *Galileo* and *Kepler*, as a result of their observations, laid the true foundations of philosophy. But it was DESCARTES who, bolder than they, meditated and made a revolution. The system of occasional causes, the idea of reducing everything to matter and movement, constituted the essence of this lively philosopher, and presuppose an analysis of ideas of which the Ancients had provided no example at all.

In shaking off the yoke of their authority, he still did not challenge sufficiently the knowledge which he had first received from them. It is astonishing that a man who ventured to question everything he had learned did not seek to follow the progress of his new knowledge from his first sensations. One might say that he was frightened by the solitude in which he had put himself, and that he was unable to endure it. All at once

94

he throws himself back into the very ideas of which he had been able to divest himself. He conjures up, as did the Ancients, pure abstractions; he regards his ideas as realities. He invents for them causes which are proportionate to their scope. He is seduced by these ancient preconceptions even while he is combating them. If I were not held back by the respect and gratitude due to such a great man, I would compare him to Samson, who, in pulling down the temple of Dagon, was crushed beneath the ruins.

The members of his sect attributed our errors to illusions of the senses, and the exaggerated zeal with which they attacked the senses had a good effect. In trying to work out the way in which our senses deceive us, men learned to analyse the way in which they give us an account of external objects. *Locke* succeeded in carrying this analysis much further, and *Berkeley* and *Condillac* followed him. They are all the children of Descartes.

When *Descartes* looked at nature, it was as if he cast a piercing glance at it, encompassed it completely, and took as it were a bird's-eye view of it.

NEWTON examined it in more detail. He described the country which the other had discovered.

Some people have made it their business to sacrifice the reputation of Descartes to that of Newton. They have imitated those Romans who, when one emperor succeeded another, simply knocked off the head of the first and substituted for it that of the second. But in the Temple of Glory there is room for all great geniuses. A statue can be erected for everyone who is worthy of it.

In between these two mighty geniuses, there happened what always happens in every field. A great man opens up new paths for the human mind. For a certain period all men are still only his pupils. Little by little, however, they level the paths which he has mapped out; they unite all the parts of his discoveries; they bring together and catalogue their valuable and authoritative features, until a new great man rises up, who soars as high above the point to which his predecessor had led the human race as that predecessor did above the point from which he set out.

NEWTON, without the experiments of *Richer*, would perhaps not have dreamed that his principles would lead him to give the world the shape of a spheroid. The greatest genius is never tempted to go deeply into theory unless he is stimulated by the facts. It is rare for men to give themselves up to reasoning. There are people who have the need to feel, but a more pressing need is required before they venture to make a leap forward.

It is said that M. *Frenicle* suspected that gravity, which made bodies fall to the ground, also kept the planets in their orbits. But from such a vague and uncertain idea to that piercing perspective, that vision of genius of *Newton*, which penetrated the immensity of the combinations and relationships of all the heavenly bodies, to that unyielding boldness which feared neither the profundity of calculation nor the beauty and difficulty of the problems, and which rose so far as to put into its balance the sun, the stars, and all the forces of nature – that is the distance from Frenicle to Newton.

Descartes discovered the art of putting curves into equations. *Huigens*, and above all Newton, suddenly carried the torch of reason into the abyss of the infinite.

Leibnitz, mighty genius and conciliator, wanted his works to become a kind of centre where all human knowledge would be united. He wanted to gather together into one bundle all sciences and all opinions. He wanted to resuscitate the systems of all the ancient philosophers, like a man trying to build a proper palace from the ruins of all the buildings of ancient Rome. He wanted to make of his Theodicy what Peter made of St Petersburg.

We owe to these great men the pattern and the laws of analysis, the lack of which had for such a long time retarded the progress of metaphysics, and even that of physics.

It could be said that there is one general respect in which these two sciences both differ from those which are called mathematical. All sciences, no doubt, have their origin in the senses. But mathematics has this advantage, that it is an application of the senses which is not susceptible to error.

The necessity of measuring fields, aided by the property which space has of being itself measured in relation to the room it occupies, gave rise to the first elements of mathematics. Ideas of numbers are neither less simple, nor less familiar; it was from these few simple ideas, which are easily combined together, that the mathematical sciences were formed. Everything which is capable of being considered as a quantity may be their subject. They are only the consequences of abstract definitions which include such a small number of ideas that it is easy to encompass all of them. A chain of truths, all depending upon one another, is formed: a chain in which men have only to recognise all the steps they have taken in order to accumulate truth upon truth. These truths become more and more fruitful; the more we advance in speculation, the more we discover of those general formulae of calculation from which we can descend to particular truths by particularising the hypotheses. The truths, when they are combined, are increased in number and combined again; and from this springs a new increase, because each becomes the source of a host of truths which are no less fruitful than the first.

To the extent that the number of these known truths increased, to the extent that the properties of a greater number of shapes were investigated, their common properties were expressed in formulae and general principles which contained everything that was known. Thus even in mathematics men began by investigating a few familiar figures, a small number of properties of lines; the general principles were the work of time.

Thus, since it was believed that the best order was that in which a multiplicity of consequences was derived from one principle alone, men were obliged, in order to incorporate it in mathematical works, to recast from century to century the whole method of instruction. It was not realised that this allegedly natural order was in fact arbitrary; that in geometry, where the general relationships of figures are set out, these relationships are reciprocal; that one may equally infer the principle from the consequence, or the consequence from the principle; the equation of the ellipse can be deduced from its construction, as its construction can be deduced from its equation.

Thus, if any method is to be preferred, it is that of tracing the steps of the human mind in its discoveries, of bringing home the general axioms which spring from all the particular truths, and at the same time making known the manner in which all the preceding truths are bound up in them. Thus the picture of the progress of mathematics is like the Olympus of the poets, which was pointed towards the earth, and which, to the extent that it moved away from the earth, expanded until it touched the sky. Thus geometry has expanded up to the infinite. Particular truths lead to more and more general formulae; and even in mathematics it is from the particular to the general that one must advance.

But when the general principles are found, what rapid progress they bring about in these sciences! Algebra, the reduction of curves to equations, the analysis of the infinite! Here there is a sequence of hypothetical truths, certain for that very reason, and at the same time verified by nature, because the first hypotheses were by no means arbitrary, but based on the ideas of extent which our senses present to us, and which they present to us only because things possessing extent really exist in nature.

Mathematics sets out from a small number of ideas, and combines their relationships *ad infinitum*. It is quite the contrary in the physical sciences, where it is a question not of a sequence of ideas and relationships, but of facts and ideas which concern an object actually existing either in the past or the present (the future can only be mathematical), and the truth of which consists in the conformity of our opinions with this object.

Under the heading of physical sciences I include logic, which is the body of knowledge concerning the operations of our minds and the generation of our ideas; metaphysics, which deals with the nature and origin of things which exist; and finally physics properly so-called, which examines the mutual action of bodies upon one another, and the causes and interconnections of sensible phenomena. One could also add history, the certainty of which can never be as great, because the concatenation of events can never be as close, and because events which took place a long time ago can only with difficulty be submitted to a new examination. Nature being always consistent with itself, we may, by means of experiments, bring before our eyes once again the same phenomena, or produce new phenomena; but if the first witnesses of an event are not very trustworthy, the event must always remain surrounded by uncertainty, and its precise effects can never be known to us.

I am not speaking here of sciences like morals and politics which depend on self-love regulated by justice, which is itself only a very enlightened form of self-love. What I have said in a general way about the differences between sciences of combination and sciences of observation may be applied to them. In the latter, man cannot confine his attention to a small number of principles. He is assailed simultaneously by a whole mass of ideas, and is forced to gather them together in large numbers, because all things which exist are bound up with one another by their mutual interaction; and he is obliged at the same time to analyse these ideas carefully until he arrives at their most simple elements.

Logic is based on the analysis of language and the reduction of the images of objects to the simple sensations of which they are composed. Metaphysics was bound to feel the effects of the small amount of progress made in this analysis. Before we had analysed our sensations and understood their causes, the real uniformity of material substances was not apparent to us. A body which is blue and a body which is red are bound to appear different, and we would scarcely have been able to contemplate the conformity which they possess if the senses had not revealed bodies considered in themselves as existing outside ourselves, capable of assuming various colours and manifesting themselves with different sensible qualities. Thence the distinction between *substance* and *mode*; but this did not at first prevent men from conceiving the *modes* as so many things existing outside ourselves, even though they could not in fact exist without a subject. Thence the errors of the majority of philosophers.

There is nothing so confused among the Ancients as all these ideas of substance, essence, and matter, which were due to the absence of proper knowledge about the way in which they originated from the first sensible ideas. They were nevertheless employed in all their ambiguity. In order to explain them, how much progress had to be made in physics itself, whose errors were holding back development! – for metaphysics and physics have a mutual need of one another. How much time was necessary to discover that all sensible phenomena could be explained by shape and movement! Descartes was the first to see this truth clearly. Before him, for want of this degree of analysis, physics remained more or less confounded with metaphysics.

The errors of metaphysics relate to the manner in which we receive, through our sensations, the idea of things existing outside ourselves. It is only by relating coloured points that we create for ourselves the idea of visible extent; it is by the gathering together of a number of sensations, which produce in us the resistance of external bodies to our own, that we create for ourselves the idea of tangible extent. It is only by reasoning that we assure ourselves of the existence of the bodies which constitute the bond and common cause of the sensations associated with them; but instinct, or, if you like, the combining together of ideas derived from experience, came before reasoning, and men confused the bodies themselves with their sensible qualities. This idea was bound to lead to that obscurity in the whole of metaphysics of which I am speaking, and which is easy to understand if we consider that the judgement we pass on the existence of external objects is only the result of their relations with us, of their effects on us, of our fears, of our desires, and of the use which we make of them. Our senses being given to us only for the preservation of our lives and our welfare, sensations are simply the true signs of our ideas about these external things, which are sufficient to make us seek or avoid them without understanding their nature. Our judgements are simply the abbreviated expression of all the movements which these bodies excite in us, an expression which guarantees for us the reality of these bodies by the reality of their effect itself. Thus our judgement on external objects does not in any way presuppose the analysis of such ideas; we judge in bulk.

On the other hand it must be observed that language, in relation to metaphysics, resembles the application which is made of geometry to physics. But apart from the fact that in language, the use of which is habitual and easy, we do not always bother not to allow ourselves any contradiction, we would be able to succeed in this only by first defining all our ideas, as a result of which we would tire ourselves out in the formulation of a series of truths which had little applicability to the usage of society, which is after all the chief aim of language.

Complete meticulousness would lead to there being no contradictions in terms, and to the formulation of a chain of hypothetical truths; but that is not enough in sciences which have to be compared with real objects. Often the problems of physics (because all the elements which concur in producing the effect have not been clearly seen) lead to a result which is absolutely contrary to experience, even though there are no mathematical errors involved. Words recall rather than express ideas. Given correct logic, we can deduce consequences very effectively; but who will vouch for the causes? And if they happen to be false, how far would the very truth of the consequences become removed from reality, if men, driven by their needs to their senses and to society, were not often forced to be inconsistent? Two contradictory ideas do not look like the object; but why do they not look like it? Usually it is because they are abstract ideas whose objects have no existence at all.

In general, the principles of the sciences in which we do not wish to stray from reality can be nothing other than facts. In metaphysics, facts can be known only through the analysis of our sensations, which in relation to external causes are only the effects which indicate them. In physics, they can be known only through a profound examination of all the circumstances, which, when it is found to be impossible, comes to constitute the necessary limit of our researches. He who is familiar with only one of the coasts of a country is uncertain whether it is an island or the mainland. That is the position we are in so far as all the objects of our ideas are concerned when we begin to reflect, and it is still the position so far as a great number of them are concerned after a great deal of reflection.

This twofold confusion of language and ideas has undoubtedly had a considerable influence on physics. Men, when they began to reason about the phenomena which confronted them, at first sought for the cause itself before they had properly understood the phenomena; and since the true causes could be discovered only in the course of time, they invented false ones. Whenever it is a question of finding the cause of an effect, it is only by way of hypothesis that we can succeed, when the effect is all that is known.

We go back, as best we can, from the effect to the cause, in our endeavours to decide what is outside ourselves. Now in order to divine the cause of an effect when our ideas do not present it to us, it is necessary to invent one: we must verify a number of hypotheses and try them out. But how can we verify them? By working out the consequences of each hypothesis and comparing them with the facts. If all the facts which are predicted on the basis of the hypothesis are found in nature precisely as the hypothesis would lead us to expect, this conformity, which cannot be the effect of chance, becomes its verification, in the same way that one identifies the seal which has made an impression when one sees that all the characteristics of the latter are included in those of the seal.

Such was the course of the progress of physics. Facts which were poorly understood, poorly analysed, and few in number were bound to lead to the invention of totally false hypotheses; the necessity of making a host of suppositions, before finding the true one, was bound to produce many. Further, the difficulty of deducing the consequences of these hypotheses and comparing them with the facts was in the beginning very great. It was only by the application of mathematics to physics that men were able from those hypotheses, which are only combinations of what necessarily happens when certain bodies are moved according to certain laws, to infer the effects which necessarily followed from them; and thereafter research was bound to increase with time. The art of making experiments, too, was perfected only in the course of time; fortunate accidents, which nevertheless happen only to those who often have these objects before their eyes and who understand them; and, much more commonly, a multiplicity of refined theories and little systems relating to details, often aided once again by mathematics – apprised men of the facts, or indicated to them the experiments which ought to be carried out together with the way to make them successful. Thus we see how the progress of mathematics supported that of physics, how everything is bound up together, and at the same time how the need to examine all the hypotheses necessitated a host of mathematical investigations which, by multiplying truths, increased the generality of the principles, thereby leading to the development of a considerable facility in calculation and the perfection of this art.

From all this it may be concluded that men were bound to pass through a thousand errors before arriving at the truth. Hence that host of systems, each one less sound than the other, which nevertheless represent real progress, real gropings towards the truth; systems, moreover, which give rise to research and are for this reason useful in their effects. Hypotheses are not harmful: all those which are false destroy themselves. The so-called systematic classifications which are really only arbitrary dictionaries would seem on the whole to check the advance of natural history, by treating it as if it were complete, whereas it can never in fact be so; and nevertheless these systems themselves represent progress. Pliny is no more scholarly a naturalist than Linnaeus; on the contrary, he falls far short of him. But Pliny was familiar with fewer objects, and fewer relations between these objects. Linnaeus is more aware of the extent to which his account is overburdened with detailed lists of objects, and of the fact that in order to identify them one must understand their relationships. He often looks for arbitrary ones – well, they will give way to the knowledge of the imperceptible gradations which unite the species. The first step is to find a system; the second is to become disgusted with it.

Let us go back to our physical hypotheses, whose diversity, as we see, is necessary, and whose uncertainty does not prevent us from being able in the end to find the true ones, at any rate when the details of the facts can be sufficiently ascertained. But besides the difficulty of analysing the facts and developing the hypotheses, there is in the manner in which they have been formed another source of error which is still more considerable. This is the only too tempting taste for analogy; ignorance sees resemblances everywhere, and unfortunately it is ignorance which passes judgement.

Before men were conversant with the mutual interconnection of physical effects, nothing was more natural than to suppose that these were produced by intelligent beings, invisible and resembling ourselves; for what else would they have resembled? Everything that happened, without men having a hand in it, had its god, in respect of whom fear or expectation soon led to the establishment of a cult; and this cult was once again devised on the model of the respect which people might have for powerful men. For the gods were only more powerful men, more or less perfect according to whether they were the product of a century which was more or less enlightened about the true perfection of humanity.

When the philosophers had recognised the absurdity of these fables, without yet having acquired any real understanding of natural history, the idea struck them to explain the causes of phenomena by way of abstract expressions like *essences* and *faculties*: expressions which in fact explained nothing, and about which men reasoned as if they were *beings*, new gods substituted for the old ones. Following these analogies, *faculties* were proliferated in order to provide a cause for each effect.

It was only much later, through observation of the mechanical action which bodies have upon one another, that men derived from this mechanics other hypotheses which mathematics was able to develop and experiment to verify. That is why physics did not cease degenerating into bad metaphysics until a long period of progress in the arts and in chemistry had multiplied the combinations of bodies, and until, with the development of closer communications between societies, geographical knowledge had become more extensive, the facts had become more certain, and the practice of the arts had itself been brought to the attention of the philosophers. Printing, literary and scientific journals, and the transactions of Academies increased the degree of certainty until today it is only the details which remain in doubt.

There is another kind of progress of the human mind, less recognised and acknowledged, but nevertheless real – that which is relative to the arts of taste, to painting, poetry, and music. Whatever the admirers of antiquity say about this, we have become more knowledgeable about these arts, without having surpassed or even attained in the arts of design that sublime beauty of which Greece (over a very short period) provided the models.

Since it is nevertheless very difficult to apprehend true taste without being arbitrary, and since its nature can be easily dulled by all kinds of habits, it has been subject to a large number of revolutions. Painting depends upon imitation; architecture was at first subject only to the method of building which convenience dictated. The techniques of these two arts were perfected, but eccentric fashions brought about variations in taste. That delicacy of feeling upon which the perfection of taste depends is not associated with either barbarism or laxity. It depends upon an elegance of manners, upon a temperate luxury which does not hinder the spread of enlightenment, but which is sufficient to ensure a market for pleasing objects and the employment of second-rate artists, among whom the great artists who shine out from them are formed. No art can continue to exist unless it succeeds in employing a number of men sufficient to carry it on as a simple craft.[1] Extravagant luxury, where vanity causes

---

[1] The English for many years have spared nothing to acquire beautiful pictures; and their nation has still not been able to produce a single great painter.

The Italians, the French, and the Flemish, and a very small number of Germans and Spaniards, have been the only ones to be successful in this art. The reason for this is that the English pay only for good pictures. By banning images from the churches, they deprived themselves of the means of supporting bad painters, and even second-rate ones. And in all crafts where bad workers cannot gain a livelihood, and second-rate workers are not comfortably off, great men are not created. Our painters of Notre-Dame bridge, who supply all the little village churches with pictures, constitute an indispensable nursery for the rearing of a few great painters. When starting in an art one is hardly assured of success in it. Thus if one had to be certain of rising to the highest rank in a craft in order to get one's bread, fathers would never set their children to it.

That is why among the English there is only a very small number of painters. Nearly all the Dutch painters have painted only landscapes, seascapes, or rustic scenes; and I do not believe that one can name a single painter of history who is at all well-known who was not a Catholic. *Author's Note.*

ornaments to be accumulated because it regards them less as ornaments than as symbols of affluence, smothers taste. Men no longer seek for the pleasure which things afford to the senses and the mind; they no longer search their own hearts. They no longer listen to anything but fashion. The sure way to judge badly in any sphere is not to judge with one's eyes. When each individual judges, the multitude judges well, because its judgement is that of a large number of people; but when no one does anything but listen, the multitude judges badly. Another cause of bad taste was often the progress of technique in the arts. Men are always liable to mistake the difficult for the beautiful. Arts, virtues – everything is infected by this error; hence the false virtues of many philosophers.

Only after a very long time did it become known that virtue among men, as well as beauty in the arts, depended on certain relationships between objects and our organs. The intellect naturally delights in apprehending these relationships, and the arts are perfected when they have reached this point. Artistic techniques, when they are perfected, appear as merits in the worker who thinks of demonstrating his dexterity, and who does not think at all about the manner in which objects ought to please, which is difficult to elucidate when one does not apprehend it with a kind of instinct. Hence Gothic architecture, which is abandoned only when antiquity is taken as a model, that is, the period when men had felt this inspiration.

Greece, too, had lost good taste, which shows that it is not barbarism alone that smothers it; but it was less conscious that it had lost it, because it had not had to endure that period of palpable barbarism which warned Europe to look for models in happier times.

With regard to painting and sculpture, since these two arts are very difficult, they were bound to fall into a decline as soon as the protection of enlightened princes came to be lacking. Not even sales in the churches, nor individual luxury, could keep them going, for individuals were impoverished: and because of the paucity of trade in all parts of Europe there was little choice. The taste which is formed through the repeated comparison of beautiful things is lost when trade between nations does not put them before one's eyes. The dauber on the corner is enough for those who enjoy only an unrefined luxury. Moreover, painting is an art which is undertaken for money and which requires genius, and the forms of government in Europe, degrading as they did everyone who was not a gentleman, reduced it to pure technique. As for Greece, it was too broken and too ravaged, both by the instability of its monarchy and by the invasions of the Saracens and the Bulgarians, to be able to cultivate the agreeable arts with success. However, it contributed to the revival of Rome in the fourteenth century through the enthusiasm which it inspired for antiquity.

There were parts of the arts of taste which could be perfected with time, for example perspective, which depends on optics. But local colour, the imitation of nature, and the expression of the passions itself are of all times. Thus those great men who at all times have pushed art forward to a certain point, acquire, in relation to the following centuries, a certain equality, and as a result they are in a way more fortunate than philosophers, who necessarily became out of date and useless through the progress of their successors.

Great men in the fields of eloquence and poetry have the same immortality, and in a way a still more lasting one, because their works are perpetuated and multiplied by means of copies. Their progress depends on languages, on circumstances, on manners, and on the chance which causes several great geniuses to arise in a nation.

One point about eloquence should be noted – that when we speak of its progress and its decline, we are thinking only of studied eloquence, of set speeches; for at all times and among all peoples, the passions and public affairs have produced men who were truly eloquent.

The histories are full of examples of powerful and persuasive eloquence in the depths of barbarism. Cardinal de Retz was more eloquent in Parliament than in the pulpit. See also Segesta, Arminius, and Vibulinus in Tacitus.

I am not at all surprised at the fall of eloquence in Greece and Rome. After the division of Alexander's empire, the kingdoms which were established on its ruins eclipsed all the small republics in which eloquence had shone with such brilliance. Alexandria and Antioch became the centres of commerce and the arts. Athens was no longer anything but a town in Greece without any authority, where young men were still sent to study, but where talent did not lead to a large fortune. Ambitious people were found at the Court of Kings, where what was necessary was not eloquence but intrigue. What took place in the public square in Athens no longer gave an impetus to the whole of Greece.

When one reads the speeches of Demosthenes, one finds that there were scarcely any which he was able to deliver in that debased and degenerate Athens. Clever teachers, whatever talents and whatever taste one may suppose them to have possessed, were thus unable to preserve true eloquence there.

They brought it about that young people, as still happens in our colleges, were presented with *amplifications* on all kinds of subjects. Nothing is more liable to distort the mind and even to destroy sincerity of character; an honest heart is not warmed by cold. Eloquence is a serious art, which persons of real worth will never play at. A man of genius will never make a parade of eloquence and waste his time in inveighing against Tarquin or Sylla, or in trying to persuade Alexander to live in peace. Thus we see that after the fall of the republics there were declaimers but no longer orators. In Rome, where the same causes had led to the same effects, several emperors, who were in love with eloquence and who condescended to engage in the composition of a number of discourses, failed to produce any Ciceros because they failed to reproduce the circumstances which had given birth to them. Men are never eloquent when they have nothing to say. They must have someone who is to be moved or convinced.

Our bar does not lend itself, or seldom lends itself, to bursts of eloquence. Cicero, accusing or defending a citizen before a popular assembly or a Roman senate invested with legislative power, could give himself up to his genius. But when it is a question of examining in a tribunal whether, according to the law, a certain inheritance should belong to Peter or to James, all that is required is a quite simple didactic tone. All that is required is to establish the truth; and any discourse which does nothing but establish the truth is not capable of giving pleasure when one has no personal concern with the subject.

As soon as political matters no longer came within the province of orators, the ancients did not know where to find a place for eloquence. They did not have the resource which we find in a great number of philosophical and moral problems which with us have given birth to a kind of eloquence which we call academic, and which, in order to achieve the success of which it is capable, still requires that those who engage in it should never indulge in *amplifications*.

The pulpit, which has carried eloquence to the highest point, has been known only to the moderns. The grandeur of God, the majestic obscurity of the mysteries, the pomp of religion, and the powerful interest of the life to come, have opened up a huge field for the sublime and moving genius of the Bossuets and the Saurins. The grandeur of the subject has even in a way given shape to another kind of florid eloquence employed by Fléchier and Massillon, who are certainly much more eloquent than Lysias and Isocrates, without attaining to the great bursts of eloquence of Bossuet.

It is perhaps surprising that the ancient Fathers did not in the same way seize this opportunity to bring about a revival of eloquence among the Greeks and the Romans. It is true that we find in some of them, and above all in the Greeks, some admirable traits. *Salvianus*, speaking to the inhabitants of Treves who after their city's revolution were demanding gladiatorial games, is not far below the level of Demosthenes who similarly reproached the Athenians for their love of entertainments. But in general these traits of the Fathers were rooted out by the power of their subject. Their discourses, which they put in the form of homilies, always had something didactic about them which was more fitted to instruct than to move. Often a love of simplicity led them to pay no heed to nobility of imagery and the other ornaments of discourse. It would appear that *St Augustine* often sought to be eloquent. Sometimes he succeeded in this: but his beauties of style were swamped beneath a deluge of witticisms and frivolous conceits into which he was drawn by the bad taste of his century, and which he had picked up in his profession as a teacher of rhetoric.

What is called bombast is, so to speak, nothing but a counterfeit of the sublime. True eloquence employs the boldest and most lively figures; but these must be produced as the result of real enthusiasm. One never moves without being moved; and the language of enthusiasm has this in common with that of all the passions, that it is ridiculous when it is only imitated, because it is always only imperfectly imitated.

An arrow which is correctly shot ascends to the target and sticks to it; if it is aimed higher it falls to the ground – an illustration of a natural figure and an extravagant one.

The intermingling of languages puts them into a state of continuous movement until their analogy is determined; and during the very time when they are changing they are softened, until great writers become the models to judge of their purity. Before this coming together, languages are never in a settled state. It is obvious that when two languages whose constructions are different come to intermingle, time will be necessary before a uniform whole results. Further, bookmen wish to retain the old language, and speak it badly because they speak it only from books; the people without books speak an unrefined language, devoid of rules and harmony; there is no more poetry in either the one language or the other; or, if a few verses are made, since it is unrefined men who make them, the verses are barbarous. It should be noted that among peoples who through time have advanced in the arts and made a certain amount of progress in ideas, the common people are more ignorant than the leading citizens even of a still-barbarous nation. Further, the mechanical arts and the subjection of the people cause minds to deteriorate. Men's first ideas have a certain analogy with the imagination and the senses, which abstract ideas, together with the progress of philosophy, cause them to lose. No doubt these new ideas are capable of being reconciled with the imagination, but new progress is required to bring this about.

Good poets do not emerge, and taste and elegance do not begin to be formed, until languages have acquired a certain richness, and above all until their analogy becomes stable. Nearly all languages are a mixture of several languages. In so far as they are intermingled, the result will consist partly of one and partly of the other. During this time of fermentation, conjugations, declensions, and the ways in which words are formed have nothing settled about them. Constructions are encumbered, and thought is obscured as a result of this encumbrance. Further, the half-formed technical languages frequently change. Poetic terms cease to be in use shortly after their invention, so that poetic language cannot grow richer. Once the language has been formed, there begin to be poets who use it. But it becomes stabilised only when it has been used in the writings of a number of great geniuses, because only then is there a point of comparison from which to judge of its purity. It is perhaps a misfortune for languages to be stabilised too soon, for so long as they are changing, they are all the time being softened and perfected.

The only cause of change in languages which are not being mixed at all with others is the establishment of metaphors, which become familiar and allow their metaphorical sense to be forgotten when they are used frequently and over a long period by writers. We know that the majority of the words which express objects which do not come directly within the purview of our senses are really metaphors derived from sensible things: for example, *penser*, *délibérer*, *contrition*, etc. Yet these words, when we hear them spoken today, no longer constitute metaphors. They appear to us only as the direct signs of some of our abstract ideas. Several of them have lost all the connections which they originally had with objects of the senses.

It is certain that those who heard a similar expression from the lips of its inventor were necessarily aware of the metaphor which it involved. Their minds, accustomed as they were to link expressions to ideas of sensible objects, must have needed to make a certain effort in order to give it a new meaning. But through its being repeated in the new sense which had been given to it, this sense became as it were appropriate to it; in order to understand it in its new meaning there was no longer any need to recall its old one. The use of the memory became all that was necessary in order to understand it; weak imaginations, which always constitute the majority, saw in it only the sign of a purely abstract idea, and passed it on to their successors on that footing.

I admit that this could lead us to fear that all those beautiful expressions which we admire in our poets may thus come to lose their charm, and that the flowers gathered by men of genius, as a result of passing through so many common hands, may one day wither. Then those who were born with the same talents would be obliged, in order to present their ideas with the same vigour, to invent new turns of phrase and new expressions, which would soon be subject to the same process of decline; and in the course of these revolutions the language of Corneille and that of Racine would become out of date, and people would no longer appreciate the charm of their poetry.

In spite of this reasoning, I think that the example of the Greek language ought to reassure us. From Homer to the fall of the Empire of Constantinople, during more than two thousand years, it did not appreciably change. Men have always been alive to the beauties of Homer and Demosthenes: the few Latin words which crept into the Greek language were far from altering it fundamentally. The critics, it is true, can tell roughly the century in which the works were written. But this is more or less solely by referring to this small number of foreign words, and still more often to the nature of the things concerned or the allusions made by the authors to different events.

I would say the same thing about Latin, in spite of the very common presumption that it was altered by the intermingling of the language of the Romans with those of the conquered nations. This is in fact so far from being true, that in the Latin authors who wrote while the Empire was in existence one can hardly find more than a few turns of phrase and a few words borrowed from barbarous languages; moreover, nearly all these words are terms relating to the arts, or names of dignities or new arms which never constitute the basic elements of a language. It all too often happens that the genius of a language is confused with the taste of those who speak it.

Claudian no doubt had very different tastes from *Virgil*, but their language was the same.

We are told that after the century of Leo X the *Cavalier Marin* substituted a puerile affectedness for the elegance of the Italian language. It is true that this is the character of his works, but it is quite false to say that he made it peculiar to his language; and I am sure that the Metastasios and Maffios, and so very many others who brought back good taste and the love of simplicity to Italy, found no obstacle in the genius of their language.

In general, a difference in style between authors who are separated from one another by several centuries no more proves that there is a difference in their languages than does the difference which is found between authors of the same period, and which is often just as great. It is not at all the difference in words and turns of phrase, but that in genius, which makes the writers of the dark ages so inferior.

The reasoning which gives rise to these reflections is valid only in the passing of the words of one language into another, and in the different revolutions undergone by a language which is a long way from being stabilised. It is then that the expressions which pass from mouth to mouth have for those who receive them only the sense given to them by those who transmit them, without their original and proper sense being preserved. But it is not the same when a language is stabilised. The books which have stabilised it always remain in existence, and, since the proper sense of the word is not lost, the metaphor is never deprived of its true meaning. Then it is not simply the ideas of the people of one generation which are passed to the following generation; the works of good authors are a storehouse in which they are preserved for ever, and to which all generations go in order to borrow them.

Languages may be stabilised so far as their analogy is concerned, and have great writers, a long time before they are enriched; for it is only the intermingling of languages which prevents them from being stabilised, and good writers resist this effect of the intermingling of languages, as happened in Greece in relation to Latin, and in relation to the oriental languages. The period of the stabilisation of languages at a point more or less near to their perfection has a great influence on the genius of nations in relation to poetry and eloquence. All the peoples whose languages are poor, the ancient Germans, the Iroquois, and the Hebrews (proof that this is not the result of climate) express themselves in metaphors. In the absence of a fixed sign for an idea, people made use of the name of the idea which was nearest akin to it, in order to make what they wanted to say understandable. The imagination struggled to find resemblances between objects, guided by the clue of a more or less exact analogy. One finds in the most civilised languages traces of these unrefined metaphors which necessity, more ingenious than fastidious, introduced into them. When the mind becomes familiar with the new idea, the word loses its metaphorical sense. I have no doubt that we could find many metaphors in the oriental languages of which those who speak them are quite unaware, and that this would be reciprocal. It must be acknowledged that the ancient languages admit metaphors which are bolder, that is, in which the analogy is less perfect, at first through necessity and later through habit. Moreover, metaphors sown in a smaller field strike us more. We have as lively an imagination as the orientals; or at any rate it would not be disputed that the Greeks and the Romans had as lively a one as the ancient peoples of the north; but since the minds of the Greeks and the Romans, and our own, are filled with a host of abstract ideas, the languages of the Greeks and the Romans, and our own, are less burdened with figures.

It follows that these languages are also more fitted to express with greater exactitude a much greater number of truths. If a language which is stabilised too soon may retard the progress of the people which speaks it, a nation which attains stability too quickly may for a similar reason find that the progress of its sciences is arrested. The Chinese were stabilised too soon. They became like those trees whose trunk has been lopped and whose branches grow close to the ground; they never escape from mediocrity. There was so much respect among them for their barely sketched-out sciences, and they retained so much for the ancestors who had caused these first steps to be taken, that it was believed that nothing remained to be added, and that it was no longer a question of anything but preventing this wonderful knowledge from being lost. But to limit oneself to preserving the sciences in their existing state is equivalent to deciding to perpetuate all the errors they contain.

The manifold investigations of men of letters which the Chinese administration is pleased to undertake necessarily restrict their minds to the matters which are their object. No longer is anything learned; no longer is anything invented. To venture in this way to mark out the roads which genius must follow, it would have been necessary to know its course; and this is something which one can never ascertain exactly, since one knows only what has been discovered, and not what remains to be discovered. The protection given to the sciences in the kingdoms of the Orient is what has caused their ruin: by burdening them with rites and transforming them into dogmas, it has restricted their progress and even caused them to move backwards. Greece so greatly surpassed the Orientals in the sciences which it obtained from them only because it was not subject to a single despotic authority. If it had been constituted, like Egypt, as a single state body, a man like Lycurgus, in order to protect the sciences, would have claimed to regulate research by administrative means. The sectarian spirit, which was quite natural for the first philosophers, would have become the spirit of the nation. If the legislator had been a disciple of Pythagoras, the sciences of Greece would have been confined for ever to the knowledge of the dogmas of that philosopher, which would have been erected into articles of faith. He would have been what the celebrated Confucius was in China. Fortunately the situation in which Greece found itself, divided up as it was into an infinity of small republics, allowed genius all the freedom and all the competition of which it has need in its endeavours. The perspectives of men are always very narrow in comparison with those of nature. It is much better to be guided by the latter than by imperfect laws. If the sciences have made such great progress in Italy, and consequently in the rest of Europe, they undoubtedly owe this to the situation in which Italy found itself in the fourteenth century, which was rather similar to that of ancient Greece.

The sciences were always regarded as mysterious among the Asiatics; and wherever sciences are *mysteries* it is rare for them not to degenerate into superstitions. Genius is never attached exclusively to certain families, or to certain places; to concentrate the sciences there is to alienate them from almost all those who are capable of perfecting them. Moreover, it is very difficult for men, the majority of whom are second-rate, once they have received the truth or the sciences as an inheritance, not to regard them as if they were an estate, a capital from which they ought to draw interest. In their hands they become the object of a shameful traffic and a vile monopoly, a kind of commodity which they further corrupt by the absurd intermixture of the most ridiculous opinions. This was the fate of the early discoveries made in the Orient, which were put in the custody of the priests. There they were debased to the point where they were no longer anything but a monstrous collection of fables, of magic, and of the most extravagant superstitions.

All these absurdities, incorporated under Alexander's successors into the ancient philosophy of the Greeks, produced the modern Pythagorism of Iamblichus, Plotinus, and Porphyrius.

We see from this that a precocious maturity, whether in the sciences or in languages, is not an advantage to be envied. Europe, slower in its progress, has borne more nourishing and more fertile fruit. The instrument which the Greek and Latin languages, and our modern languages, have offered to it, and offer to us, is more difficult to handle. But it is capable of being applied to a much greater number of uses and tasks. The multiplicity of abstract ideas which our languages express, and which enter into our analogies, demand great dexterity in their employment. That is the disadvantage of perfected languages. There are more words which are not the bearers of images at all. Thus it needs more skill and talent to paint portraits in these languages, which have become so suitable for defining and demonstrating. But for the great geniuses this very difficulty, which exercises their talent and obliges them to put forth their strength, leads them to successes of which the infancy of languages and nations was not capable. The first painters in Greece used only three colours: their pictures were able to show feeling. But Raphael could draw as well as they could, and Guido Reni, Titian, and Rubens, with the thousand colours with which they loaded their palettes, achieved a fidelity to nature of which the Ancients could have no idea. In the same way Greek and Latin, by giving sonorous terminations to the old, hard roots of the Asiatic languages, and our modern languages by giving them to those of the peoples of the north, have promoted harmony; and the multiplicity of analogies has given birth to happy turns of phrase which have afforded number and variety to style.

From this arises the beauty especially of Greek and Latin poetry, which were able, owing to the particular constitution of their analogy, to look after inversions and to make use of the quantity of syllables in order to create their rhythm, while almost all other nations were reduced, in order to mark out the metre perceptibly, to have recourse to rhyme. Poetry, once brought to perfection in these languages, became truly a kind of painting, although one would have believed at first sight that the metaphorical languages of the Orient would have painted with more brilliance and force. Nothing of the kind: these languages paint readily, but crudely and badly, without propriety and without taste.

The sciences, which are based on the combination or the knowledge of objects, are as boundless as nature. The arts, which are only relations to ourselves, are as limited as we are; in general all those which are carried on to give pleasure to the senses have a point which they are unable to pass, determined by the limited sensibility of our organs. They are a long time in reaching this point. For example, it is only lately that music has reached its perfection, and, indeed, perhaps it has not yet done so. Moreover, it is wrong to criticise those who want to advance further: if they go beyond the mark, our senses are bound to give us warning of this. Poetry, indeed, in so far as it harmoniously renders images which are full of elegance, will go no further than Virgil. But although perfect in this respect and in relation to style, it is capable of continuous progress in many other respects. The passions will not be painted more effectively, but variations in circumstances will mean that their activity has new effects. The art of combining all the circumstances and directing them to our interest, the verisimilitude and choice of characters, and everything which pertains to the composition of the works, will be capable of being perfected. Ever more dexterity will be acquired as the result of experience. By means of a great amount of subtle reflection, men will learn the way in which one should go about giving pleasure. They will know how to make pleasing garlands from those flowers which nature gave to all the Ancients and which she has not denied to us. In the long run the unceasing imitation of the great models, even their faults, will often preserve their successors from the lapses which sometimes mar the most sublime writings. The progress of philosophy, of all branches of physical knowledge, and of history, which at every moment brings new events on to the world scene, will provide writers with those new subjects which are the food of genius.

There is another cause of variations in taste: manners have a powerful influence on the choice of ideas, and it would consequently appear that the peoples whose society was in the most flourishing condition must have had a more exquisite taste. Taste consists in properly expressing graceful or powerful ideas. Everything which is neither fact, nor feeling, nor image, languishes. Hence in part the disadvantage of languages which are advanced and rich in abstract ideas; it is easier to chatter in them, if I may put it like that, and less easy to paint in them. Reflection is the remedy for this defect, for whatever our pedants say about it, we have become more simple in our century. Transportation is now despised: a strange difference between our progress and that of the Ancients! The leading men among them were too unrefined; among us they are too subtle. This arises from the fact that their taste was formed at the same time as their ideas, but we had ideas before we had any taste.

In general, taste may be bad either as a result of the choice of vile, base, and tedious ideas – and wealthy peoples, to the extent that their society is more cultivated, learn to avoid these; or else as a result of images which are not sensible enough. Let me explain. In the pleasure which comparisons give us there are two pleasures: one is that of the mind which connects two ideas; the other, and unquestionably the greater, is that which arises from the very agreeableness of the images which are presented to it. All the images of things which speak to the imagination and the heart, and which give pleasure to the senses, beautify style and imbue it with that charm with which nature has endowed the things which surround us and which constitute the source of our wellbeing; the sensitive soul is moved by them. But mathematical images, those figures which are indeed in nature, but do not form part of that living nature which alone is connected with us through the bond of pleasure – these images do not bear anything with them except barrenness. The relations may be just as true, but they are more difficult to grasp and say nothing to the heart. This is one of the great differences between intellect and genius. The latter, based as it is on sensibility, is able to choose images capable of putting the soul into that state of happy perturbation which affords visions of the beauties of nature. That is why so many new combinations of matter which our modern discoveries have put before our eyes have so little enriched our poetry: it is because all these ideas, although sensible, give no pleasure to our senses, or at any rate there are very few which have this advantage. Thus it is an effect of the progress of philosophy to put more intellect into style and to render it colder. One must also avoid pushing even the most graceful ideas of nature to the point of anatomical detail where their pleasure is lost; it is in this way alone that intellect can displease. I believe that the language of a people, once it has been formed and stabilised by great writers, no longer changes. Thus I think that the decline of letters in Italy and in Greece came only after a period much longer than we are told, and that poetry then fell into the same state of decline as all other studies, this being the result of the very decline of manners in the Empire. So far as eloquence is concerned, I have given the reason elsewhere.

The Ancients, because they were ancients, were sheltered from pedantry. We know how harmful to taste the vain display of erudition has at all times been.

To want to preserve admiration for the great models by establishing a taste which excludes new forms – that is to behave like the Turks, who did not know how to preserve the virtue of their women except by keeping them in prison. Must one always admire, without producing anything? Pedantry of this kind destroyed Greek literature under the Roman empire.

There are minds which nature has endowed with a memory capable of assembling together a large number of pieces of knowledge, and a power of exact reasoning capable of comparing them and arranging them in a manner which puts them in their full light; but to whom at the same time she has denied that fire of genius which invents and which opens up new paths for itself. Created to unite the discoveries of others under a point of view fitted to clarify and perfect them, if they are never torches which shine with their own light, they are diamonds which brilliantly reflect a borrowed light, but which in total darkness would be confounded with the meanest stones. These minds are necessarily the last to arrive.

It is not necessary to believe that in times of weakness and decline, or even in those of barbarism and darkness which sometimes succeeded centuries of the greatest brilliance, the human mind made no progress. The mechanical arts, commerce, and the usages of civil life gave birth to a host of reflections which were diffused among men, which were mingled with education, and which constantly grew in quantity as they passed from generation to generation. They pave the way slowly, but profitably and surely, for happier times: like those rivers which are hidden beneath the ground during a part of their course, but which reappear further down, swollen by large quantities of water which have seeped through all those parts of the soil which the current, as determined by the natural gradient, has passed through without showing itself.

The mechanical arts have never suffered the same eclipse as letters and the speculative sciences. An art, once it has been invented, becomes an object of commerce which is self-sustained. There is no need to fear that the art of making velvet will be lost so long as there are people to buy it. The mechanical arts thus continue to exist when letters and taste have fallen, and if they continue to exist, they are perfected. No art whatever can be cultivated during a long succession of centuries without passing through the hands of several inventive minds. We also see that in spite of the ignorance which prevailed in Europe and in the Greek empire after the fifth century, the arts were enriched by a thousand new discoveries without any of the slightest importance being lost.

The art of navigation was perfected, and also the art of commerce. To these centuries we owe the habitual use of bills of exchange, the science of keeping commercial books which is the most perfect form of accounting, the cotton paper invented in Constantinople and the rag paper invented in the west, window glass, plate glass and the art of making mirrors, spectacles, the compass, gunpowder, windmills and water-mills, clocks, and an infinite number of other arts unknown to antiquity.

Architecture offers us an example of the reciprocal independence of taste and mechanical operations in the arts. There are no buildings at all which are in worse taste than Gothic structures; and there are none at all which are more durable, or whose construction demanded more vigour and more practical knowledge of the methods of carrying it out, although these methods could only be the result of a multitude of tentative attempts, since the mathematical sciences were then in their infancy, and the thrust of the arches and roofs could not be calculated with precision.

It was necessary that these arts should be cultivated and perfected in order that real physics and the higher philosophy could be born. They brought the carrying out of exact and conclusive experiments within reach. Without the invention of the telescope, we would never have been able to work out the causes of the movements of the heavenly bodies. Without that of the suction-pump, we would never have been able to discover the heaviness of air.

Let us be careful, therefore, not to confuse success in the mechanical arts with artistic taste, or even with the speculative sciences.

Artistic taste can be lost as the result of a multitude of purely moral causes. The diffusion of a spirit of apathy and softness in a nation, pedantry, contempt for men of letters, eccentricity in the taste of princes, tyranny, and anarchy can corrupt it.

It is not the same with the speculative sciences. So long as the language in which books are written continues to exist, and so long as a certain number of men of letters still remain, nothing that is known is forgotten. It is true that the sciences are then not perfected, because there are few men and consequently few geniuses who apply themselves to them; but they are not completely lost.[1] Also, the Greek teachers of rhetoric who went to Italy after the taking of Constantinople knew everything which had been known in ancient Greece. All that they lacked was taste and the critical faculty. They were simply scholars.

The inundations of the barbarians in the east had a more fatal effect. By destroying the Latin language, they caused the knowledge of the books written in that language to be lost. We would no longer have them, if the monks had not preserved a part of them.

The arts continued to exist in spite of this general calamity. Blows more violent than this are needed in order to overthrow them. It was only the Turks who, in the ferocity of their conquests, were able to cause them to retreat. This must be attributed less to their religion, which did not prevent the Moors of Spain from being very enlightened for their time, than to the nature of their despotism of which we have spoken above, and to the complete separation of the nations made subject to their empire – a separation which kept up a war of hatred in the state, and a balance of oppression and revolt. Brought up in *harems*, abodes of softness and of an authority at the same time ignorant and absolute which could only degenerate into habitual cruelty, the Turks had no industry and knew nothing but violence. The Greeks, bent under a yoke of the harshest kind, lived in fear of it all the time. The enervated Turks, and the

[1] The revolutions which bring about the fall of eloquence and taste in the fine arts, without wiping out the memory of the sciences or preventing a certain amount of cultivation of them, are like the fires which sometimes devastate forests. One can still find a few half-formed trunks remaining alive, but stripped of their branches and their leaves, without flowers and without adornment. *Author's Note.*

oppressed Greeks, both in a state of uncertainty as regards their position, their goods, and their lives, could not think of easing an existence which was so disturbed and so little theirs. Consequently there were no arts at all, apart from those which were absolutely indispensable; and among the others, the few which had been preserved in the seraglio were reduced to techniques without any taste.

The invention of printing spread not only the knowledge of books, but also that of the modern arts, and it has greatly perfected them. Before its invention, a host of admirable techniques, which tradition alone passed on from one craftsman to the other, excited no curiosity at all among the philosophers. When printing had facilitated their communication, men began to describe them for the use of the craftsmen. Through this, men of letters became aware of a thousand ingenious operations of which they had been ignorant, and they found themselves led towards an infinity of notions which were full of interest for physics. It was like a new world, in which everything pricked their curiosity. Thus was born a taste for experimental physics, in which great progress could never have been made without the help of inventions and technical processes. . .

Afterword by Du Pont

It would seem that this work was never completed. M. Turgot regarded it only as a *sketch*. But although he did not put the finishing touches to it, in which he would perhaps have extended or contracted part of the meta-physical observations, subtle and profound as they are, which are mixed up with his historical views, we have thought fit neither to suppress nor to mutilate an essay which contains such a large number of philosophical truths, often expressed with so much elegance and genius.

Reflections on the Formation and the Distribution of Wealth

৵৻৶

FIRST

Impossibility of Commerce on the assumption of an equal division of land,
where each man would have only what was necessary
for his own support.

If the land were distributed among all the inhabitants of a country in such a way that each of them had precisely the quantity necessary for his support, and nothing more, it is evident that, all being equal, no one would be willing to work for others. Also no one would have the means of paying for the labour of another; for each man, having only as much land as was necessary to produce his own subsistence, would consume all that he had gathered in, and would have nothing which he could exchange for the labour of others.

II

The above hypothesis has never existed, and could not have continued to
exist. The diversity of soils and the multiplicity of needs lead
to the exchange of the products of the land for other products.

This hypothesis could never have existed, because the lands were cultivated before being divided, cultivation itself having been the only motive for the division and for the law which secures to every man his property. The first men who engaged in cultivation probably cultivated as much land as their resources would permit, and consequently more than was necessary for their own support.

Even if this state of affairs could have existed, it could not have been a lasting one. If each man drew no more than his subsistence from his land, and did not have the means of paying for the labour of others, he would not be able to meet his other needs for housing, clothing, etc. except by means of his own labour, and this would be virtually impossible, since *all land falls far short of producing everything.*

The man whose land was suitable only for corn, and would produce

119

neither cotton nor hemp, would lack cloth with which to clothe himself. Another man would have land suitable for cotton which would produce no corn. One would lack wood to keep himself warm, while another would lack corn to feed himself. Experience would soon teach each man the kind of product for which his land was most suitable; and he would confine himself to cultivating this, in order to procure for himself the things which he lacked by means of exchange with his neighbours, who, having in their turn reasoned in the same way, would have cultivated the produce best suited to their land and abandoned the cultivation of all others.

III

The products of the land require long and difficult preparations in order to render them suitable to meet men's needs.

The produce which the land yields in order to satisfy the different needs of men cannot for the most part serve to do this in the state in which nature affords it; it must be subjected to various changes and be prepared by means of art. Wheat must be converted into flour and then into bread; hides must be tanned or dressed; wool and cotton must be spun; silk must be drawn from the cocoons; hemp and flax must be soaked, peeled, and spun; then different fabrics must be woven from them; and then they must be cut and sewn in order to make them into clothing, footwear, etc. If the same man who caused these different things to be produced from his land, and who used them to meet his needs, were also obliged to subject them to all these intermediate preparations, it is certain that the result would turn out very badly. The greater part of these preparations demand an amount of care, attention, and long experience which is acquired only by working continuously and on a great quantity of materials. Take for example the preparation of hides. Where is the husbandman who could attend to all the details involved in this operation, which goes on for several months and sometimes for several years? If he could, would he be able to do it for a single hide? What a loss of time, space, and materials, which could have served at the same time, or successively, to tan a great number of hides! And even if he did succeed in tanning one single hide, he needs only one pair of shoes: what would he make out of the remainder? Shall he kill an ox in order to have this pair of shoes? Shall he cut down a tree to make himself a pair of clogs? The same may be said of all the other needs of each man, who, if he were reduced to his own land and his own labour, would involve himself in a great deal of time and trouble in order to be very badly equipped in every respect, and would cultivate his land very badly.

IV

The necessity for these preparations leads to the exchange of products for labour.

The same motive which brought about the exchange of one kind of produce for another as between the Cultivators of soils of different qualities was bound to lead also to the exchange of produce for labour as between the Cultivators and another part of society, which had come to prefer the occupation of preparing and working up the products of the land to that of growing them. Everyone gained as a result of this arrangement, for each man by devoting himself to a single kind of work succeeded much better in it. The Husbandman obtained from his land the greatest possible quantity of products, and by means of the exchange of his surplus procured for himself all the other things he needed much more easily than he would have done by means of his own labour. The Shoemaker, by making shoes for the Husbandman, appropriated to himself a portion of the latter's harvest. Each Workman worked to meet the needs of the Workmen of all the other kinds, who in their turn all worked for him.

V

Pre-eminence of the Husbandman who produces over the Artisan who prepares. The Husbandman is the prime mover in the circulation of men's labour ; it is he who causes the land to produce the wages of all the Artisans.

It must however be noted that the Husbandman, who supplies everyone with the most important and considerable objects of their consumption (I mean their food and also the materials of almost all manufactures), has the advantage of a greater degree of independence. His labour, among the various kinds of labour which are shared out between the different members of society, retains the same primacy and the same pre-eminence that the labour which provided for his subsistence possessed among the different kinds of labour which he was obliged, when he was in a solitary state, to devote to his needs of all kinds. What we have here is a primacy arising not from honour or dignity, but from *physical necessity*. The Husbandman, generally speaking, can get on without the labour of the other Workmen, but no Workman can labour if the Husbandman does not support him. In this circulation, which by means of the reciprocal exchange of needs renders men necessary to one another and constitutes the bond of society, it is therefore the labour of the Husbandman which is the prime mover. Whatever his labour causes the land to produce over and above his personal needs is the unique fund from which are paid the wages which all the other members of society receive in exchange for their labour. The latter, in making use of the consideration which they receive in this exchange to purchase in their turn the produce of the Husbandman, do no more than return to him exactly what they have received from him. Here we have a very basic difference between these two kinds of labour, and before we deal with the innumerable consequences which spring from it we must dwell upon it in order that we may be fully aware of how self-evident it is.

VI

The wage of the Workman is limited to his subsistence as a result of competition between Workmen. He earns no more than a living.

The simple Workman, who possesses only his hands and his industry, has nothing except in so far as he succeeds in selling his toil to others. He sells it more or less dear; but this higher or lower price does not depend upon himself alone; it results from the agreement which he makes with the man who pays for his labour. The latter pays him as little as he is able; since he has a choice between a great number of Workmen he prefers the one who works most cheaply. Thus the Workmen are obliged to vie with one another and lower their price. In every kind of work it is bound to be the case, and in actual fact is the case, that the wage of the Workman is limited to what is necessary in order to enable him to procure his subsistence.

VII

The Husbandman is the only one whose labour produces anything over and above the wage of the labour. He is therefore the unique source of all wealth.

The position of the Husbandman is quite different. The land, independently of any other man and of any agreement, pays him directly the price of his labour. Nature never bargains with him in order to oblige him to content himself with what is absolutely necessary. What she grants is proportionate neither to his needs nor to a contractual evaluation of the price of his working day. It is the physical result of the fertility of the soil, and of the correctness, much more than of the difficulty, of the means he has employed to render it fruitful. As soon as the labour of the Husbandman produces something over and above his needs, he is able, with this surplus over and above the reward for his toil which nature affords him as a pure gift, to purchase the labour of other members of the society. The latter, when they sell to him, earn no more than their living; but the Husbandman obtains, besides his subsistence, an independent and disposable form of wealth, which he has never purchased but which he sells. He is therefore the unique source of all wealth, which, through its circulation, animates all the industry of society; because he is the only one whose labour produces anything over and above the wage of the labour.

VIII

Primary division of society into two classes: first, the productive *class, or the Cultivators; and second, the* stipendiary *class, or the Artisans.*

Here then we have the whole society divided, as the result of a necessity founded on the nature of things, into two classes, both of which are occupied in work. But one of these, through its labour, produces or rather extracts from the land wealth which is continually renascent, and which provides the whole of society with subsistence and the materials for all its needs. The other, engaged in preparing the produced materials and giving them forms which render them suitable for men's use, sells its labour to the first, and receives its subsistence from it in exchange. The first may be called the *productive* class, and the second the *stipendiary* class.

IX

In the earliest times the Proprietor could not have been distinguished from the Cultivator.

Up to now we have made no distinction at all between the Husbandman and the Proprietor of the land; and in the beginning they were not in fact distinguished at all. It was as a result of the labour of those who first worked the fields, and who enclosed them, in order to make certain of securing the harvest, that all the land ceased to be common to all and that landed property was established. Until societies were consolidated, and until public power, or the law, having come to predominate over individual power, was able to guarantee everyone the peaceful possession of his property against all invasion from without, one could maintain one's ownership of a piece of land only in the way that one had acquired it, and by continuing to cultivate it. It would not have been safe to have one's fields worked by another who, having undergone all the toil involved, would have had difficulty in understanding that the whole of the harvest did not belong to him. Moreover, in these early times every industrious man would be able to find as much land as he wanted, and could thus not be induced to till the soil for others. Every proprietor was obliged either to cultivate his fields or to abandon them completely.

X

Progress of society; all land comes to have an owner.

But the land became populated, and was brought into cultivation to a greater and greater extent. In the course of time all the best land came to be occupied. There remained for the last comers only the infertile soils which had been rejected by the first. But in the end all land found its owner; and those who could not possess properties had at first no course open to them other than to exchange the labour of their hands in the occupations of the *stipendiary* class for the surplus produce of the cultivating Proprietor.

XI

It begins to be possible for the Proprietors to shift the labour of cultivation on to paid Cultivators.

But since the land rendered the owner who cultivated it not only his subsistence, not only the means of procuring for himself by way of exchange the other things he needed, but also a large surplus, he was able with this surplus to pay men to cultivate his land. And for men who live on wages, it is just as good to earn them in this occupation as in any other. Thus ownership could be separated from the labour of cultivation, and soon it was.

XII

Inequality in the division of property: causes which make this inevitable.

The original Proprietors, as has already been said, at first occupied as much land as their resources allowed them and their families to cultivate. A man of greater strength, more industrious, and more anxious about the future took more land than a man with the opposite character. He whose family was larger, having more needs and more hands, extended his possessions further; here was already a first form of inequality. All land is not equally fertile: two men with the same area of land and the same labour may obtain very different products from it: a second source of inequality. Properties, in passing from fathers to children, are divided up into portions which are more or less small according to whether the families are more or less numerous. As one generation succeeds another, the inheritances at one time are further subdivided, and at another time are brought together again through the dying out of branches of the family: a third source of inequality. The contrast between the intelligence, the activity, and above all the thrift of some with the indolence, inactivity, and extravagance of others, constituted a fourth cause of inequality, and the most powerful one of all. The negligent and improvident Proprietor, who cultivates badly, and who in abundant years consumes the whole of his surplus in frivolities, on the occurrence of the slightest accident finds himself reduced to asking for help from his more prudent neighbour, and to living on loans. If, as the result of new accidents or the continuation of his negligence, he finds that he is not in a position to pay, and if he is obliged to have recourse to new loans, there will in the end be nothing left for him to do but abandon a part or even the whole of his estate to his creditor, who will take it as an equivalent; or to part with it to another in exchange for other assets with which he will discharge his obligation to his creditor.

XIII

Consequence of this inequality: the Cultivator distinguished from the Proprietor.

So here we have landed estates as objects of commerce, being bought and sold. The portion of the Proprietor who is extravagant or unfortunate serves to increase that of the Proprietor who is luckier or more prudent; and in the midst of this infinitely varied inequality of possessions it is impossible that a great number of Proprietors should not possess more than they are able to cultivate. Moreover it is natural enough that a wealthy man should wish to enjoy his wealth in peace, and that instead of employing all his time in arduous labour he should prefer to give a part of his surplus to people who will work for him.

XIV

Division of the product between the Cultivator and the Proprietor.
Net product *or revenue.*

According to this new arrangement, the product of the land is divided into two parts. One comprises the subsistence and profits of the Husband-man, which are the reward for his labour and the condition upon which he undertakes to cultivate the Proprietor's fields. What remains is that independent and disposable part which the land gives as a pure gift to the one who cultivates it, over and above his advances and the wages of his toil; and this is the share of the Proprietor, or the *revenue*, with which the latter is able to live without working and which he takes wherever he wishes.

XV

New division of the Society into three classes, the Cultivators, the Artisans, and the Proprietors, or the 'productive' class, the 'stipendiary' class, and the 'disposable' class.

So now we have the Society divided into three classes: the class of Husbandmen, for which we may keep the name *productive class*; the class of Artisans and other *stipendiaries* supported by the product of the land; and the class of *Proprietors*, the only one which, not being bound by the need for subsistence to one particular kind of work, may be employed to meet the general needs of the Society, for example in war and the administration of justice, whether through personal service, or through the payment of a part of its revenue with which the State or the Society may hire men to discharge these functions. The name which for this reason suits it best is the *disposable class.*

XVI

Resemblance between the two industrious or non-disposable classes.

The two classes of Cultivators and Artisans resemble one another in many respects, and above all in the fact that those of whom they are composed do not possess any revenue and live equally on the wages which are paid to them out of the product of the land. Both also have this in common, that they earn nothing but the price of their labour and of their advances, and this price is almost the same in the two classes. The Proprietor beats down those who cultivate his land in order to give up to them the smallest possible portion of the product, in the same way as he haggles with his Shoemaker in order to buy his shoes as cheaply as possible. In a word, neither the Cultivator nor the Artisan receive more than a recompense for their labour.

XVII

Essential difference between the two industrious classes.

But there is this difference between these two kinds of labour, that the Cultivator's labour produces his own wage, and in addition the revenue which serves to pay the whole class of Artisans and other stipendiaries, whereas the Artisans receive simply their wages, that is, their share of the product of the land, in exchange for their labour, and do not produce any revenue. The Proprietor enjoys nothing except through the labour of the Cultivator; he receives from him his subsistence and the means of paying for the work of the other stipendiaries. He has need of the Cultivator because of a necessity which arises from the physical order of things, by virtue of which the land produces nothing at all without labour; but the Cultivator has need of the Proprietor only by virtue of human conventions and the civil laws which guaranteed to the original Cultivators and their heirs the ownership of the land which they had occupied, even after they ceased to cultivate it. But these laws could guarantee to the man who took no part in the work himself only that part of the product which the land yields over and above the recompense due to the Cultivators. The Proprietor is forced to abandon the latter, on pain of losing the whole. The Cultivator, completely restricted though he is to the recompense for his labour, thus retains that natural and physical primacy which renders him the prime mover of the whole machine of Society, and which causes not only his own subsistence, but also the wealth of the Proprietor and the wages for all other kinds of work, to depend upon his labour alone. The Artisan, on the other hand, receives his wages, either from the Proprietor or from the Cultivator, and gives them, by the exchange of his labour, only the equivalent of these wages and nothing over and above this.

Thus, although neither the Cultivator nor the Artisan earn more than a recompense for their labour, the Cultivator generates over and above this recompense the revenue of the Proprietor, and the Artisan does not generate any revenue, either for himself or for others.

XVIII

This difference justifies their being distinguished as the productive *class and the* sterile *class.*

Thus we may distinguish the two non-disposable classes as the *productive class*, which is that of the Cultivators, and the *sterile class*, which includes all the other stipendiary members of the Society.

XIX

How the Proprietors are able to derive a revenue *from their land.*

The Proprietors who do not work their land themselves may adopt various methods of getting it cultivated, or make various arrangements with those who cultivate it.

XX

First method : cultivation by men who are paid wages.

In the first place they may pay men by the day or by the year to work their fields, reserving for themselves the whole of the product. This presupposes that the Proprietor makes the advances both for the seed and for the wages of the workmen until after the harvest. But this first method has the drawback of requiring a great deal of labour and attention on the part of the Proprietor, who alone can direct the workmen in their labours, and keep an eye on the use of their time and on their trustworthiness so that none of the product is misappropriated. It is true that he may also pay a man of greater intelligence, and with whose trustworthiness he is familiar, to direct the workmen and keep an account of the product in the capacity of overseer or manager; but he will always run the risk of being deceived. Moreover, this method is extremely expensive, unless a large population and the lack of employment in other kinds of work forces the workmen to content themselves with very low wages.

XXI

Second method : cultivation by Slaves.

In times bordering on the origin of Societies, it was virtually impossible to find men who were willing to work the land of others, because all the land was not yet occupied, and those who wished to work preferred to break in new land and cultivate it on their own account. This is pretty much the position in which men find themselves in all new Colonies.

Violent men then conceived the idea of obliging other men by force to labour for them. They used slaves. The latter can look for no justice from people who could not have reduced them to slavery without violating all the rights of humanity. Yet the physical Law of nature still assures to them their share of the products which they cause to be brought forth, for the master must necessarily feed them in order to profit by their labour. But this kind of recompense is limited to the barest necessities and to their subsistence.

This abominable custom of slavery was once universal, and is still spread over the greater part of the earth. The main object of the wars which the ancient Peoples waged with one another was to carry off Slaves, whom the Conquerors forced to labour for their benefit or sold to others. This banditry and this trade still prevail in all their horror on the coasts of Guinea, where they are fomented by the Europeans who go there to buy Negroes for the cultivation of the American Colonies.

The excessive labour which avaricious masters force their slaves to perform causes many of them to perish; and it is necessary, in order that the number required for cultivation should always be kept up, that trade should annually supply a very great quantity of them. And as it is always war which constitutes the main means of supplying this trade, it is obvious that it can continue to exist only so long as men are divided into very small Nations which constantly rend one another, and each village makes war on its neighbour. Let England, France, and Spain wage the most furious war with one another: it would be only the frontiers of each State which would be invaded, and that only at a small number of points. The whole of the remainder of the country would remain quiet, and the small number of prisoners which could be taken on one side or the other would constitute a very inadequate source of supply for cultivation in any of the three Nations.

XXII

Cultivation by slaves cannot continue to exist in great Societies.

Thus, when men gather together in great Societies, the slave-recruits cease to be sufficiently abundant to provide the number consumed by cultivation. And although the lack of men's labour is made up for with that of cattle, there comes a time when the land is no longer capable of being worked by slaves. The use of them is retained only for domestic service, and at length it dies out completely, because as Nations become civilised they enter into mutual agreements for the exchange of prisoners of war. These agreements are arrived at the more easily, as each individual is greatly concerned to avert the danger of his falling into slavery.

XXIII

Slavery to the soil succeeds slavery properly so-called.

The descendants of the first slaves, originally bound to the cultivation of the land, themselves undergo a change of condition. A state of internal peace among the Nations results in trade no longer being supplied with the means of providing for an excessive consumption of slaves, so that the masters are obliged to treat them with more consideration. Those who are born in the house, as they are accustomed from infancy to their condition are less rebellious about it, and the masters have less need to employ severe measures in order to keep them in check. Little by little the land which they cultivate becomes their fatherland. They have no other language than that of their masters; they become part of the same Nation; familiarity ensues, and as a result trust and humanity on the part of the masters.

XXIV

Vassalage succeeds slavery to the soil, and the slave becomes proprietor.
Third method : alienation of the estate subject to the
payment of dues.

The management of a property cultivated by slaves is an arduous task which involves close attention and an irksome restriction on one's place of abode. The owner ensures himself of a freer, easier, and more secure enjoyment of his property by interesting his slaves in cultivation and giving up to each of them a certain area of land, on condition of their rendering to him a portion of its fruits. Some made this bargain for a period of time, and afforded to their *serfs* only a precarious and revocable possession. Others gave up the land in perpetuity, reserving for themselves an annual rent, payable in produce or in money, and requiring of the possessors the performance of certain duties. Those who received their land under the condition prescribed became proprietors and free, under the name of *tenants* or *vassals*; and the former proprietors, under the name of *seigneurs*, retained only the right of exacting the payment of the rent and the other stipulated duties. This is the way in which things have gone in the greater part of Europe.

XXV

Fourth method: the Métayer *system.*

These estates, having become free subject to the payment of rent, may again undergo a change of Proprietors, and be divided and united again as a result of successions and sales; and such and such a *Vassal* may in his turn come to have more land than he can cultivate himself. As a rule the rent to which the land is subject is not high enough to prevent one who cultivates it well from still procuring for himself, over and above the advances, the costs, and the Cultivator's subsistence, a surplus of produce which constitutes a revenue: and thus the *Vassal* proprietor too is bound to wish for the enjoyment of this revenue without involving himself in any trouble, and to have his land cultivated by others. Moreover, the majority of the Seigneurs alienate only those parts of their possessions which are least within their scope, and keep those which they can have cultivated at less cost. Cultivation by slaves being no longer practicable, the first method which presented itself, and the most simple, to induce free men to cultivate land which did not belong to them, was to give up to them a share of the fruits; this induced them to cultivate the land better than workmen on fixed wages would do. The most common division was into two equal parts, of which one belonged to the Husbandman and the other to the Proprietor. This is what gave rise to the name of *Métayer* (*medietarius*), or Husbandman with half the produce. In arrangements of this kind, which are to be found throughout the greater part of France, the Proprietor makes all the advances of cultivation, i.e., he provides at his own expense the labouring cattle, the ploughs and other implements of husbandry, the seed, and the subsistence of the Husbandman and his family from the moment when the latter enters on the *métairie* until after the first harvest.

XXVI

Fifth method : tenant-farming, or the letting-out of Land.

Intelligent and wealthy Cultivators, who suspected to what heights the fertility of the land could be raised by means of active and well-managed cultivation, in which neither labour nor expense were spared, correctly judged that they would gain more if the Proprietor consented to give up to them, for a certain number of years, the whole of the harvest, on condition of their paying him every year a fixed revenue and making all the advances required for cultivation. Through this, they would be assured that the increase in products which their expenditure and their labour caused to be brought forth would belong to them in its entirety. The Proprietor for his part gained from it a more peaceful enjoyment of his revenue, since he was relieved of the trouble involved in making the advances and in keeping an account of the products; a more regular enjoyment of it, since he received every year the same price for his farm; and a more certain enjoyment, because he never ran the risk of losing his advances, and because the live-stock and other effects with which the Farmers had stocked his farm became a security which assured him of payment. Moreover, since the lease was only for a few years, if his Farmer had given too low a price for his land he could increase it at the expiry of the lease.

XXVII

This last method is the most advantageous of all, but it presupposes a country which is already wealthy.

This method of putting out land to lease is the most advantageous of all to the Proprietors and to the Cultivators; it becomes established in all places where there are wealthy Cultivators in a position to make the advances involved in cultivation; and as wealthy Cultivators are in a position to provide the land with much more labour and manure, there results from it a huge increase in the product and the revenue of landed property.

In Picardy, Normandy, the environs of Paris, and in the majority of the Provinces of the North of France, the land is cultivated by Farmers.

In the Provinces of the South they are cultivated by *Métayers*; therefore the Provinces of the North of France are incomparably more wealthy and better cultivated than those of the South.

XXVIII

Recapitulation of the different methods of turning land to account.

I have just enumerated five different methods by which Proprietors have been able, in exempting themselves from the labour of cultivation, to turn their estates to account by means of the hands of others.

The first, by workmen paid fixed wages.

The second, by slaves.

The third, by giving up the estate for a rent.

The fourth, by giving up to the Cultivator a particular share, usually one-half, of the fruits, the Proprietor undertaking to make the advances involved in cultivation.

The fifth, by letting out the land to Farmers who undertake to make all the advances involved in cultivation, and who bind themselves to pay the Proprietor, for the number of years agreed upon, an unvarying revenue.

Of these five methods, the first is too expensive, and is very rarely put into use; the second can find a place only in countries which are still ignorant and barbarous; the third is less a method of turning one's property to account than a surrender of one's property in return for a debt claim on the estate, so that the old Proprietor, properly speaking, is no more than a creditor of the new one.

The two last methods of cultivation are those most generally used: that is, cultivation by *Métayers* in poor countries, and cultivation by Farmers in more wealthy countries.

XXIX

Of capitals in general, and of the revenue of money.

There is another way of being wealthy without working and without possessing land of which I have not yet spoken. It is necessary to explain its origin and its relation with the rest of the system of the distribution of wealth in society, of which I have just sketched the outlines. This way consists in living on what is called the revenue of one's money, or on the interest which is derived from money put out on loan.

XXX

Of the use of gold and silver in commerce.

Silver and gold are two commodities like others, and less valuable than many others since they are of no use for the real needs of life. In order to explain how these two metals have become the pledge representing all kinds of wealth, what influence they exercise in the business of commerce, and how they enter into the composition of fortunes, we must go back a little and retrace our steps.

XXXI

Birth of Commerce. Principle of the valuation of exchangeable things.

Reciprocal need led to the introduction of the exchange of what one possessed for what one did not possess; men exchanged one kind of produce for another, and produce for labour. In these exchanges it was necessary that the two parties should agree about the quality and the quantity of each of the things that were exchanged. In this agreement it is natural that each should desire to receive as much and to give as little as he can; and since both are equally masters of what they have to give in the exchange, it is up to each of them to balance the attachment he has for the commodity he gives against the desire he has for the commodity he wants to receive, and in accordance with this to fix on the quantity of each of the things exchanged. If they are not in agreement, they will have to draw nearer one another by yielding a little on both sides, offering more and contenting themselves with less. Let us suppose that one of the parties is in need of corn and the other of wine, and that they agree to exchange *one bushel of corn* for *six quarts of wine*. It is obvious that each of the parties regards *one bushel of corn* and *six quarts of wine* as exact equivalents, and that in this particular exchange the price of *one bushel* of corn is *six quarts* of wine, and the price of *six quarts* of wine is *one bushel* of corn. But in another exchange between other men this price will be different, according to whether one of the parties has a more or less urgent need for the other's commodity; and *one bushel* of corn will possibly be exchanged for *eight quarts* of wine, while in another case *one bushel* will be exchanged for only *four quarts*. Now it is obvious that no one of these three prices any more than another can be regarded as the true price of the bushel of corn, since for each of the contracting parties the wine which he received was the equivalent of the corn which he gave: in a word, so long as we consider each exchange as isolated and standing on its own, the value of each of the things exchanged has no other measure than the need or the desire of the contracting parties, balanced on one side and the other, and is fixed by nothing but the agreement of their will.

XXXII

How the current value comes to be established in the exchange of commodities.

However, it often happens that several Individuals have wine to offer to the man who has corn: if one of these is not willing to give any more than *four quarts* for a *bushel*, the Proprietor of the corn will not give him his corn if he comes to learn that someone else will give him *six quarts* or *eight* for the same *bushel*. If the first man wants to have corn, he will be forced to raise the price to the level of the one who offers more. The Sellers of wine gain on their side from the competition between the Sellers of corn: no one decides to part with his commodity until he has compared the different offers that are made to him of the commodity which he needs, and he gives preference to the highest offer. The value of corn and wine is no longer haggled over by two isolated Individuals with reference to their reciprocal needs and resources; it is fixed as a result of the balancing of the needs and resources of the whole body of Sellers of corn with those of the whole body of Sellers of wine. For someone who would willingly give *eight quarts* of wine for *one bushel* of corn will in fact only give *four* if he comes to learn that a Proprietor of corn is willing to give *two bushels* of corn for *eight quarts*. The price which represents an average between the different offers and the different demands will become the current price to which all the Buyers and Sellers will adapt themselves in their exchanges; and it will be true to say that *six quarts* of wine are the equivalent of *one bushel* of corn for everyone if that is the average price, until a lowering of offers on one side or of demands on the other brings about a change in this valuation.

XXXIII

Commerce gives to each commodity a current value, relative to each of the other commodities, from which it follows that every commodity is the equivalent of a certain quantity of every other commodity, and may be regarded as a pledge which represents it.

Corn is exchanged not only for wine, but also for all the other things which the proprietors of corn may need – for wood, leather, wool, cotton, etc.; and what applies to wine applies to every other particular commodity. If *one bushel* of corn is the equivalent of *six quarts* of wine, and *one sheep* is the equivalent of *three bushels* of corn, this same *sheep* will be the equivalent of *eighteen quarts* of wine. The man who has corn and needs wine may without disadvantage exchange his corn for a sheep, in order afterwards to exchange this sheep for the wine that he needs.

XXXIV

Each commodity can serve as a scale or common measure with which to compare the value of all others.

It follows from this that in a country where Commerce is very brisk, where there are many products and much consumption, and where there are many offers and demands for all kinds of commodities, each kind will have a current price relatively to every other kind; that is, a certain quantity of one will be equivalent to a certain quantity of each of the others. Thus the same quantity of corn which is worth eighteen quarts of wine will also be worth one sheep, one piece of dressed leather, and a certain quantity of iron; and in commerce all these things will have an equal value. To express and make known the value of any particular thing, it is clear that it is sufficient to state the quantity of any other known commodity which would be regarded as its equivalent. Thus in order to make known what a piece of leather of a particular size is worth, we may say indifferently that it is worth *three bushels of corn* or *eighteen quarts of wine*. In the same way we may express the value of a certain quantity of wine by the number of sheep or bushels of corn which it is worth in Commerce.

We see by this that all the different kinds of commodities that can be objects of Commerce measure one another, so to speak; that each may serve as a common measure or scale of comparison to which to relate the values of all the others; and in like manner each commodity becomes, in the hands of the one who possesses it, a means of procuring all the others, a kind of universal pledge.

XXXV

Every commodity does not present an equally convenient scale of values. Preference was bound to be given in practice to those which are not susceptible to any great difference in quality and thus have a value which is in the main relative to their number or quantity.

But although all commodities essentially possess this property of representing all the others, of being able to serve as a common measure to express their value, and as a universal pledge for procuring all of them by means of exchange, not all can be employed with the same facility for these two purposes. The more a commodity is susceptible to changes in value when its quality changes, the more difficult it is to make it serve as a scale to which to relate the value of other commodities. For example, if *eighteen quarts* of *Anjou* wine are the equivalent of *one sheep, eighteen quarts* of *Cape* wine may be equivalent of *eighteen sheep.* Thus one who, in order to make known the value of a sheep, should say that it was worth eighteen quarts of wine would be using language which was equivocal and conveyed no precise idea, unless he added a lengthy explanation, which would be very inconvenient. So men were bound to choose for their scale of comparison, in preference to others, those commodities which, being more commonly in use and thus having a more generally known value, were more like one another, and whose value was therefore more relative to their number or quantity than to their quality.

XXXVI

Failing an exact correspondence between value and number or quantity, people make up for it by means of an average valuation which becomes a sort of ideal money.

In a country where there is only one breed of sheep, the value of a fleece or that of a sheep can easily be taken as the common measure of values, and people will say that a barrel of wine or a piece of material is worth a certain number of fleeces or sheep. It is true that there is some disparity between sheep, but when it is a question of selling sheep care is taken to evaluate this disparity, and to reckon, for example, two lambs as equal to one sheep. When it is a question of valuing any other commodity, people take as their unit the common value of a sheep of average age and average condition. In this way, the statement of values in terms of sheep becomes as it were a conventional language, and the words *one sheep* in the language of commerce simply signify a certain value which in the minds of those who hear them convey the idea not only of a sheep but also of a certain quantity of each of the more common commodities which are regarded as the equivalent of this value; and this expression will end up by referring to a fictitious and abstract value rather than to a real sheep; with the result that if by chance a large number of sheep die, so that in order to get one it becomes necessary to give twice as much corn or wine as one formerly gave, people will say that *one sheep* is worth *two sheep* rather than alter the expression for all other values to which they have become accustomed.

XXXVII

Examples of these average valuations which become an ideal expression of values.

The commerce of every Nation presents us with quite a number of examples of these fictitious valuations in terms of commodities which are only, so to speak, a conventional language for the expression of their value. Thus the Cooks of Paris and the Fishmongers who supply large establishments generally sell *by the piece*. A fat pullet is reckoned as one piece; a chicken as half a piece, more or less according to the season, and so on. In the trade of Negro slaves to the American Colonies, a cargo of Negroes is sold at the rate of so much per head of Negro, an *Indes piece.* The women and children are valued in such a way that, for example, three children, or one woman and one child, are reckoned as one head of Negro. The valuation is increased or diminished in proportion to the strength or other qualities of the slaves, so that a particular slave may be reckoned as *two head of Negro.*

The *Mandingo* Negroes, who carry on a trade in gold dust with the Arabian Merchants, relate all their commodities to a fictitious scale of which the parts are called *macutes*, so that they tell the Merchants that they will give them so many *macutes* in gold. They also value the commodities they receive in terms of *macutes*, and their haggling with the Merchants turns on this valuation. Similarly in Holland they reckon in terms of *Bank florins*, which are only fictitious money and which in commerce have sometimes a higher and sometimes a lower value than the money called *florins*.

XXXVIII

Every commodity is a pledge which is representative of all the objects of Commerce ; but it is more or less convenient in use according to whether it is more or less easy to transport and to keep without deterioration.

The variation in the quality of commodities, and in their price in accordance with this quality, which renders them more or less suitable than others to serve as a common measure, also to a greater or lesser extent stands in the way of their being a representative pledge of all other commodities of the same value. But so far as this latter property is concerned there is also a very great difference between the different kinds of commodities. It is obvious, for example, that a man who possesses a piece of cloth is much surer of being able to procure himself a certain quantity of corn when he wants it, than if he had a barrel of wine of the same value; for the wine is subject to an infinity of accidents which are capable of depriving him of the whole of its value in an instant.

XXXIX

Every commodity has the two essential properties of money, to measure and to represent all value ; and, in this sense, every commodity is money.

These two properties of serving as a common measure of all values and of being a representative pledge of all commodities of the same value, embody all that constitutes the essence and utility of what is called money; and it follows from the account I have just given that all commodities are in certain respects *money*, and share in these two essential properties to a greater or lesser extent in accordance with their particular nature. All are more or less suitable to serve as a common measure in proportion as they are in more general use, of a more similar quality, and more easy to divide into parts of equal value. All are more or less suitable to be a universal pledge of exchanges in proportion as they are less susceptible to diminution and deterioration in their quantity or quality.

XL

Conversely, all money is essentially a commodity.

One can take as a common measure of value only that which itself has a value, that which is received in Commerce in exchange for other values; and there is no pledge universally representative of a value except another of equal value. A purely conventional money is thus an impossibility.

XLI

Different articles are capable of serving and have in fact served as ordinary money.

A number of Nations have adopted as a common measure of value, in their language and in their Commerce, different articles of a more or less precious character. Even today there are certain Barbarous Peoples which make use of a type of small shell called *Cowrie*. I remember having seen at College apricot stones exchanged and passed as a kind of money among the Scholars, who made use of them in playing various games. I have already spoken of evaluation in terms of head of cattle. We find traces of this in the Laws of the ancient Germanic Nations which destroyed the Roman Empire. The early Romans, or at any rate their ancestors the Latins, also made use of it. It is asserted that the first coins which were struck in copper represented the value of a sheep, and bore the impression of that animal, and that it is from this that the word *pecunia* has come, from *pecus*. This conjecture has a great deal of probability.

XLII

The Metals, and above all gold and silver, are more suitable for this purpose than any other substance; and why.

We have now arrived at the introduction of the precious metals into Commerce. All the metals, as they have been discovered, have been accepted in exchanges in proportion to their real utility. Their brilliance has caused them to be sought for to serve as ornaments; their malleability and solidity have rendered them suitable for making vessels which are lighter and more durable than those made of clay. But these substances could not be brought into Commerce without almost immediately becoming the universal Money. A piece of any metal, of whatever kind, has exactly the same qualities as any other piece of the same metal, provided that it is equally pure: the ease with which one metal can, by different operations of Chemistry, be separated from others with which it may be alloyed, always makes it possible to reduce them to the degree of purity, or, as it is called, *to the title*, which is desired: and then the value of the metal can only vary according to its weight. Thus in expressing the value of each commodity in terms of the weight of the metal which is given in exchange for it, we have the clearest, the most convenient, and the most potentially precise expression of all values; and consequently it is impossible that it should not in practice be preferred to every other. Nor are the metals any less suitable than other commodities to become the universal pledge of all the values they are capable of measuring: since they are capable of being divided in every imaginable way, there is no object of Commerce whose value, whether great or small, cannot be exactly paid for by a certain quantity of metal. To this advantage of lending themselves to every kind of division, they add that of being imperishable; and those which are rare, like silver and gold, have a very great value in a very inconsiderable weight and bulk.

These two metals, then, are of all commodities the easiest to verify as to their quality, to divide as to their quantity, to keep for a long period without deterioration, and to transport everywhere at the least cost. Everyone who has a surplus commodity, and who is not at the moment in need of another commodity for his use, will therefore hasten to exchange it for money, with which he is more certain than with anything else to be able to procure the commodity he wants at the moment he needs it.

XLIII

Gold and silver are constituted as money, and universal money, through the nature of things, independently of any agreement and any law.

Thus we have gold and silver constituted as money, and universal money, and this without any arbitrary agreement between men, and without the intervention of any law, but through the nature of things. They are not, as many people have thought, signs of values: they themselves have a value. If they are capable of being the measure and the pledge of other values, they have this property in common with all other objects which have a value in Commerce. They differ from them only because being at once more divisible, more imperishable, and more easy to transport than the other commodities, it is more convenient to employ them to measure and to represent values.

XLIV

The other metals are employed in these uses only in a subsidiary capacity.

All the metals would be capable of being employed as money. But those that are very common have too little value in too great a bulk to be employed in the everyday exchanges of Commerce. Copper, silver, and gold are the only ones which have been brought into regular use. And even copper, except among a few Peoples whom neither mines nor Commerce have yet been able to provide with a sufficient quantity of gold and silver, has always served only in exchanges of the smallest values.

XLV

The use of gold and silver as money has increased their value as materials.

It would have been impossible for the eagerness with which everyone sought to exchange his surplus commodities for gold or silver, rather than for any other commodities, not to have greatly increased the value of these two metals in Commerce. As a result of this they have become even more suitable for their employment as pledge and common measure.

XLVI

Variations in the value of gold and silver as compared with the other objects of Commerce, and with one another.

This value is susceptible to change, and does in fact change continually, so that the same quantity of metal which used to correspond to a particular quantity of such and such a commodity ceases to correspond to it, and more or less money is required to represent the same commodity. When more is required we say that the commodity is dearer, and when less is required we say that it is cheaper; but we could just as well say that it is the money which is cheaper in the first case and dearer in the second. Not only do silver and gold vary in price when compared with all other commodities, but they also vary in price when compared with one another, in proportion to the extent that they are more or less abundant. It is well known that in Europe today we give from *fourteen* to *fifteen ounces of silver* for *one ounce of gold*, whereas in earlier times only *ten* to *eleven ounces of silver* were given for *one ounce of gold*. Even today in China they give only about *twelve ounces of silver* to get *one ounce of gold*, so that there is a very great advantage in taking silver to China in order to exchange it for gold to bring back to Europe. It is obvious that in the long run this Commerce is bound to render gold more common in Europe and more scarce in China, and that the values of these two metals must in the end be brought back everywhere into the same proportion.

A thousand different causes concur to determine at each moment the values of commodities and to cause them continually to vary when compared either with one another or with money. The same causes determine the value of money and cause it to vary when compared either with the value of each individual commodity or with the totality of the other values which are currently the subjects of Commerce. It would not be possible to disentangle these different causes and to treat of their effects without going into very extensive and very difficult detail, and I shall refrain from entering upon such a discussion.

XLVII

The practice of making payments in money gave rise to the distinction between the Seller and the Buyer.

To the extent that men became familiar with the practice of valuing everything in money, of exchanging all their surplus for money, and of exchanging money only for things which were useful or pleasing to them at the moment, they became accustomed to consider the exchanges of Commerce from a new point of view. They distinguished between two persons, the Seller and the Buyer. The Seller was the one who gave the commodity for the money, and the Buyer was the one who gave the money to get the commodity.

XLVIII

The use of money greatly facilitated the separation of different labours as between the different Members of Society.

The more that money came to stand for everything else, the more possible it became for each person, by devoting himself entirely to that type of cultivation or industry which he had chosen, to relieve himself of all worry about providing for his other needs, and to think only about how to obtain as much money as he could through the sale of his produce or his labour, in the complete certainty that with this money he would be able to get all the rest. It was in this way that the use of money prodigiously accelerated the progress of Society.

XLIX

Of the reserve of annual produce, accumulated to form capitals.

As soon as men were found whose ownership of land assured them of an annual revenue more than sufficient to meet all their needs, there were bound to be found men who, either because they were anxious about the future or merely because they were prudent, put into reserve a portion of what they gathered in each year, whether to guard against possible accidents or to increase their well-being. When the produce which they gathered in was difficult to keep, they must have sought to obtain for themselves in exchange objects of a more durable nature whose value would not be lost with time, or which could be employed in such a fashion as to obtain profits which would more than make up for the deterioration.

L

Movable wealth; accumulation of money.

Possessions of this kind, resulting from the accumulation of unconsumed annual produce, are known by the name of *movable wealth*. Furniture, houses, plate, commodities in store, the tools of each trade, and live-stock constitute wealth of this kind. It is obvious that men worked hard to obtain as much as they could of this kind of wealth, before they became acquainted with money; but it is no less clear that as soon as it became known, as soon as it was established, that money was the most imperishable of all objects of Commerce and the easiest to keep without inconvenience, it could not fail to be sought after above all other things by anyone who wanted to accumulate. It was not only the Proprietors of land who accumulated their surplus in this way. Although the profits of industry, unlike the revenues of the land, are not a gift of nature, and although the man engaged in industry gets from his labour only the price which is given to him for it by the one who pays his wages; although the latter economises as much as possible in paying these wages, and although competition forces the man engaged in industry to content himself with a price lower than he would like – it is nevertheless certain that this competition was never so extensive or so keen in all the different branches of labour as at any time to prevent a man who was more skilful, more energetic, and above all more economical than others in his personal consumption, from being able to earn a little more than was required for the subsistence of himself and his family, and from putting this surplus into reserve in order to build up a little stock of money.

LI

Movable wealth is an indispensable prerequisite for all kinds of remunerative work.

It is also necessary that in every trade the Workmen, or the Entrepreneurs who set them to work, should have a certain fund of movable wealth accumulated beforehand. Here we are again obliged to retrace our steps in order to recall a number of matters which were to begin with indicated only in passing, when we were talking about the division of the different occupations and the different means by which the Proprietors could turn their estates to account, because we could not at that stage have explained them properly without breaking the thread of ideas.

LII

Necessity of advances in cultivation.

Every kind of work, whether in cultivation, in industry, or in commerce, requires advances. Even if one should work the land with one's hands, sowing would be necessary before reaping; one would have to live until after the harvest. The more that cultivation is perfected and the more energetic it becomes, the larger are these advances. There is need of live-stock, implements of husbandry, and buildings in which to keep the live-stock and to store the produce; it is necessary to pay a number of people proportionate to the extent of the undertaking and enable them to subsist until the harvest. It is only by means of substantial advances that we can obtain rich harvests, and that the land yields a large revenue. In every trade, whatever it may be, it is necessary beforehand that the Workman should have tools, and that he should have an adequate quantity of the materials upon which he is to work; it is necessary that he should be able to subsist while waiting for the sale of his products.

LIII

First advances furnished by the land while still uncultivated.

It is always the land which is the primary and unique source of all wealth: it is the land which through cultivation produces all revenue; and it was the land which provided the first fund of advances prior to all cultivation. The first Cultivator took the seeds he sowed from plants which the earth had produced of itself; while waiting for the harvest, he lived by hunting and fishing, and upon wild fruits. His tools were the branches of trees uprooted in the forests, shaped with edged stones which he sharpened on other stones; he himself captured in the chase animals wandering in the woods, or caused them to fall into his traps; he brought them into sub-jection and domesticated them, using them at first for his food and then to assist him in his labour. This primary fund grew little by little. Live-stock, especially, were of all kinds of movable wealth the most sought after in these early times, and the kind which it was easiest to accumulate: they die, but they reproduce themselves, and the wealth embodied in them is in a way imperishable. This fund, moreover, increases simply by

147

the process of generation, and yields an annual product, in the form either of milk foods, or of wool, hides, and other materials which, together with the wood procured in the forests, constituted the first fund for the works of industry.

LIV

Live-stock, movable wealth even prior to the cultivation of land.

In a time when a large amount of land was still uncultivated and belonged to no one, it was possible to possess live-stock without being a Proprietor of land. It is even probable that men almost everywhere began to gather flocks and herds and to live on their produce before they devoted themselves to the more arduous labour of cultivation. It would seem that the Nations which were the earliest to cultivate the land were those who found in their Country species of animals which were more susceptible to domestication, and who as a result of this were led from the restless, nomadic life of Peoples who live by hunting and fishing to the more tranquil life of Pastoral Peoples. Pastoral life requires a longer period of residence in one and the same place; it affords more leisure, and more opportunity to study the differences between soils and to observe the course of nature in the production of those plants which serve for the support of live-stock. Perhaps this is the reason why the Asiatic Nations were the first to cultivate the land, and why the Peoples of America have remained for such a long time in the Savage state.

LV

Another kind of movable wealth, and of advances of cultivation : Slaves.

Slaves were another kind of movable wealth, procured at first by violent means and later by way of Commerce and exchange. Those who possessed a large number of slaves employed them not only in the cultivation of land but also in the different branches of industry. The ease with which these two kinds of wealth could be accumulated almost without limit and made use of even independently of land, made it possible to evaluate the land itself and to compare its value with that of movable wealth.

LVI

Movable wealth has an exchangeable value in relation to the land itself.

A man who had a large amount of land but no live-stock or slaves would certainly make an advantageous bargain if he surrendered a portion of his land to a man who gave him in exchange cattle and slaves to cultivate the remainder. It was mainly in this way that landed estates themselves entered into Commerce and acquired a value comparable with that of all other commodities. If *four bushels* of corn, the net product of an acre of land, were worth *six sheep*, the acre itself which produced them could be transferred at a certain value, larger than this, it is true, but always easily determined in the same manner as the price of every other commodity; that is, at first by haggling between the two contracting parties, and then in accordance with the current price which is established by the competition of those who want to exchange land for live-stock and those who want to part with live-stock to get land. It is in accordance with this current price that land is evaluated when a Debtor is sued by his Creditor and is forced to give up his estate to him.

LVII

Evaluation of land in accordance with the proportion which the revenue bears to the amount of movable wealth, or the value for which it is exchanged : this proportion is what is called the number of years' purchase of the land.

It is obvious that if a piece of land which produces a revenue equivalent to *six sheep* can be sold for a certain value, which can always be expressed by a number of *sheep* equivalent to this value, this number will bear a definite proportion to the number *six*, and will contain it a certain number of times. The price of an estate will then be simply a certain number of times its revenue; *twenty times* if the price is *120 sheep*; *thirty times* if it is *180 sheep*. Thus the current price of land is regulated by the proportion which the value of the estate bears to the value of the revenue, and the number of times that the price of the estate contains the revenue is called *the number of years' purchase of the land.* Land is sold at *twenty years' purchase*, at *thirty years' purchase, forty*, etc., when twenty, thirty, or forty times its revenue is paid in order to acquire it. It is also obvious that this price, or this number of years' purchase, will necessarily vary according to whether there is a greater or lesser number of people who want to sell or buy land, just as the price of all other commodities varies in accordance with the differing proportion between supply and demand.

LVIII

Every capital in the form of money, or every sum of values of whatever kind, is the equivalent of a piece of land producing a revenue equal to a particular fraction of this sum. First employment of capitals. Purchase of a landed estate.

Let us now go back to the period following the introduction of money. The ease with which money could be accumulated soon made it the most sought after form of movable wealth, and afforded the means of continuously increasing the quantity of it by the simple method of economy. Anyone who, whether in the form of revenue from his land, or of wages for his labour or his industry, receives each year more value than he needs to spend, can put this surplus into reserve and accumulate it: these accumulated values are what is called *a capital*. The faint-hearted Miser, who fears that he may come to lack the necessities of life in an uncertain future, amasses money only in order to set his mind at rest about this, and keeps it in a hoard. If the dangers he foresaw were realised, and he were forced through poverty to live every year on his treasure, or if a prodigal Heir were to spend it bit by bit, this treasure would soon be exhausted and the capital entirely lost to the Possessor. But the latter can make use of it in a much more advantageous way. Since a landed estate of a certain revenue is only the equivalent of a sum of values equal to that revenue multiplied a certain number of times, it follows that any sum of values whatever is the equivalent of a landed estate producing a revenue equal to a particular fraction of that sum. It is a matter of complete indifference whether this sum of values or this capital consists of a mass of metal or of any other thing, since money represents all kinds of value, just as all kinds of value represent money. The Possessor of a *capital* may therefore, in the first place, employ it in the purchase of land; but there are also other courses open to him.

LIX

Another employment of money, in the advances of manufacturing and industrial enterprises.

I have already noted that all kinds of work, whether in cultivation or in industry, required advances. And I have shown how the land, by means of the fruits and plants which it produced of itself for the nourishment of men and animals, and by means of the trees from which men formed their first tools, provided the first advances of cultivation, and even of the first hand-made products which each man might fashion for his own use. For example, it was the land which provided the stone, the clay, and the wood from which the first houses were constructed; and, before the separation of occupations, when the same man who cultivated the land provided for his other needs by his own labour, no other advances were necessary. But when a large part of Society came to have nothing but their own hands to support them, it was very necessary that those who thus lived on wages should begin by having something in advance, either to procure the materials upon which they worked, or to enable them to live while waiting for the payment of their wages.

LX

Further points about the use of capital advances in industrial enterprises, about their returns, and about the profit they ought to yield.

In the earliest times he who set men to work provided the materials himself and paid from day to day the wages of the Workman. It was the Cultivator or the Proprietor himself who gave to the Spinner the hemp he had gathered in, and maintained her while she was working: then he passed the yarn to a Weaver to whom he paid every day the agreed wage. But insubstantial daily advances of this kind can suffice only in the case of crude manual labour. A large number of Arts, and even of Arts engaged in by the poorest Members of Society, require that the same material should pass through many different hands, and undergo for a very long time very difficult and diverse preparations. I have already mentioned the preparation of the hides from which shoes are made: anyone who has seen a Tanner's works will appreciate the absolute impossibility of one poor man, or even several poor men, providing themselves with hides, lime, tan, tools, etc., getting the buildings which are necessary for the operation of a Tannery erected, and living for several months until the leather is sold. In this Art and in many others, is it not necessary that those who work at it should have learned the trade before venturing to touch the material, which they would spoil in their first attempts? Here, then, another advance is indispensable. And who, in the next place, will collect together the materials for the work, and the ingredients and tools necessary for their preparation? Who will get canals, markets, and buildings of all kinds constructed? Who will make it possible for this great number of Workmen to live until the leather is sold, when no one of them could prepare a single hide on his own, and when the profit from the sale of a single hide could not afford subsistence for any one of them? Who will defray the costs of the instruction of Pupils and Apprentices? Who will obtain for them the means of subsistence during the period until they are taught, enabling them to pass step by step from labour which is easy and proportioned to their age to tasks which require the greatest vigour and ability? It will be one of those Possessors of *capitals*, or of movable accumulated values, who will use them, partly as advances for construction and the purchase of materials, and partly as the daily wages of the Workmen who work them up. He it is who will wait until the sale of the leather returns to him not only all his advances, but also a profit sufficient to compensate him for what his money would have been worth to him if he had employed it in the acquisition of an estate, and, in addition, for the wages due for his work, his trouble, his risks, and his ability itself; for there is no doubt that if the profit were the same he would have preferred to live without any exertion on the revenue of an estate which he could have acquired with the same capital. As fast as this capital is returned to him through the sale of the products, he employs it in making new purchases in order to supply and maintain his Factory by means of this continual circulation: he lives on his profits, and he puts into reserve what he is able to save, in order to increase his capital and invest it in his enterprise, adding to the amount of his advances so as to add still further to his profits.

LXI

Subdivision of the industrial stipendiary Class into capitalist Entrepreneurs and ordinary Workmen.

Thus the whole Class which is engaged in meeting the different needs of Society with the vast variety of industrial products finds itself, so to speak, subdivided into two orders: that of the Entrepreneurs, Manufacturers, and Masters who are all possessors of large capitals which they turn to account by setting to work, through the medium of their advances, the second order, which consists of ordinary Artisans who possess no property but their own hands, who advance nothing but their daily labour, and who receive no profit but their wages.

LXII

Another employment of capitals, in the advances of Agricultural enterprises. Observations on the use, the return, and the indispensable profits of capitals in Agricultural enterprises.

In speaking first of the employment of capitals in Manufacturing enterprises, my aim was to present a more striking example of the necessity and effect of large advances, and of the process of their circulation. But in doing this I have to some extent reversed the natural order of things, which would have required me to begin by speaking about agricultural enterprises, which similarly cannot come into being or be enlarged or become profitable except through the medium of large advances. It is the Possessors of large capitals who, in order to turn them to account in agricultural enterprises, take leases of land, paying the Proprietors a high rent for it and undertaking to make all the advances of cultivation. Their situation must be the same as that of the Entrepreneurs of Factories: like them, they must make the first advances of the enterprise, provide themselves with cattle, horses, and implements of husbandry, and purchase the first seed; like them, they must maintain and feed the Carters, Reapers, Threshers, Servants, and Workmen of all kinds who possess nothing but their hands, advance nothing but their labour, and earn nothing but their wages. And like them, they must get in, over and above the return of their capital, i.e., of all the original and annual advances,

(1) a profit equal to the revenue they could acquire with their capital without any labour; (2) the wages and the price of their labour, their risks, and their industry; (3) the means of annually making up for the wear and tear of the items of property employed in their enterprise – the live-stock that die, the implements that wear out, etc. All this must be deducted from the price of the produce of the land; the surplus serves the Cultivator for paying the Proprietor for the permission the latter has given him to make use of his land for the establishment of his enterprise. This is the price of the lease, the revenue of the Proprietor, the *net product*; for everything which the land produces up to the amount of the return of the advances and the profits of every kind accruing to him who makes them cannot be regarded as a *revenue*, but only as a *return of the costs of cultivation*, since if the Cultivator did not get these back he would take good care not to employ his wealth and his toil in cultivating the land of another.

LXIII

The competition of Capitalist Entrepreneurs in agriculture establishes the current price of leases, and large-scale cultivation.

The competition of wealthy agricultural Entrepreneurs establishes the current price of leases in proportion to the fertility of the land and the price at which its produce is sold, always in accordance with the calculation which the Farmers make of their costs and of the profits which they ought to draw from their advances: they are unable to give the Proprietor more than the surplus. But when competition between them is very keen, they give him the whole of this surplus, since the Proprietor will let his land only to the man who offers the highest rent.

LXIV

The lack of Capitalist Entrepreneurs in agriculture confines the working of land to small-scale cultivation.

When, on the other hand, there are no wealthy men at all who have large capitals to put into agricultural enterprises; when, owing to the low price of the produce of the land or to any other cause, the crops are not sufficient to ensure to the Entrepreneurs, over and above the return of their capital, profits at least equal to those which they would derive from their money if they employed it in any other way, no Farmers at all will be found willing to take the land on lease. The Proprietors are forced to get it cultivated by Husbandmen or *Métayers* who are not in a position to make any advances or to carry on proper cultivation. The Proprietor himself makes scanty advances which yield him a very scanty revenue: if the land happens to belong to a Proprietor who is poor, or in debt, or neglectful, or to a widow or a Minor, it remains uncultivated. This is the true cause of the difference upon which I have already remarked between the Provinces in which the land is cultivated by wealthy Farmers, as in Normandy and the Isle of France, and those in which it is cultivated only by poor *Métayers*, as in Limousin, L'Angoumois, Le Bourbonnais, and many others.

LXV

Subdivision of the Class of Cultivators into Entrepreneurs or Farmers, and ordinary Wage-earners, Hands or Day-labourers.

Hence it follows that the Class of Cultivators, like that of Manufacturers, is divided into two orders of men, that of the Entrepreneurs or Capitalists who make all the advances, and that of the ordinary Workmen on wages. We also see that it is capitals alone which establish and maintain great Agricultural enterprises, which give the land, so to speak, an invariable rental value, and which ensure to the Proprietors a revenue which is always regular and as high as it is possible for it to be.

LXVI

Fourth employment of capitals, in the advances of Commercial enterprises. Necessity for the intervention of Merchants, properly so-called, between the Producers of commodities and the Consumers.

The Entrepreneurs, whether in agriculture or in Manufacture, get back their advances and their profits only through the sale of the fruits of the earth or of the manufactured products. It is always the needs and *the means* of the Consumer which set the price at the sale; but the Consumer does not always need the thing which is manufactured or produced at the moment when the harvest is brought in or the work finished. However, the entrepreneurs need their capitals to be returned to them immediately and regularly in order to reinvest them in their enterprises. Harvesting must be followed without a break by ploughing and sowing; the Workmen in a Manufactory must be kept continuously employed, work on new products must begin as fast as the old ones are completed, and materials must be replaced as fast as they are used up. One cannot with impunity interrupt the work of an established enterprise, and resume it again just when one wishes. Thus the Entrepreneur has the greatest possible interest in getting his capital returned to him very quickly through the sale of his crops or his products: on the other hand, the Consumer has an interest in finding the things which he needs when and where he wants them; it would be extremely inconvenient for him if he were obliged to buy his provisions for a whole year at the moment when the harvest was brought in. Among the objects of common consumption there are many which require long and costly labours, which can be profitably undertaken only upon a very large quantity of materials – so large that the consumption of a small number of men or of a district of limited area may not be sufficient to absorb the output of a single Manufactory. Enterprises where the work is of this kind, therefore, must necessarily be few in number, at a considerable distance from one another, and consequently very far from the homes of the majority of the consumers. There is no man above the level of extreme poverty who is not in a position to consume a number of things which are gathered in or manufactured only in places far removed from his home and equally far removed from one another. A man who could not obtain the objects of his consumption except by buying them directly from the hands of him who had gathered them in or manufactured them would either go without a good many things, or spend his whole life in travel.

This two-fold interest which the Producer and the Consumer have, the first in finding an opportunity to sell and the second in finding an opportunity to buy, yet without wasting precious time in waiting for a Purchaser or in seeking out a Seller, was bound to suggest to third parties that they might act as intermediaries between the one and the other. And this is the purpose of the profession of the Merchant, who buys commodities from the hands of the Producer in order to accumulate them or put them in a warehouse, where the Consumer comes to get what he wants. By this means the Entrepreneur, assured of a market and of the return of his capital, devotes himself without anxiety and without any letting-up to producing further goods, and the Consumer finds within his reach, and at any moment, the things of which he stands in need.

LXVII

Different orders of Merchants. All have this in common, that they buy in order to resell; and that their traffic depends upon advances which have to be returned with a profit, in order to be newly invested in the enterprise.

From the Woman who offers her herbs for sale in the market-place, up to the Ship-owner of Nantes or Cadiz who carries on his sales and purchases as far away as India and America, the profession of a merchant, or what is properly called commerce, is divided into an infinity of branches, and, so to speak, of degrees. One merchant confines himself to laying in a stock of one or of several kinds of commodities which he sells in his shop to all who come there. Another goes and sells particular commodities in a place where they are lacking, in order to bring back from there in exchange commodities which are produced there and which are lacking in the place from which he set out. One makes his exchanges in his own neighbour-hood and by himself; another through the medium of Correspondents, and by the agency of Carriers whom he pays, sends out, and causes to go from one Province to another, from one Kingdom to another Kingdom, from Europe to Asia, and from Asia to Europe. One sells his commodities in small portions to each of the individuals who consume them; another sells only large quantities at a time to other Merchants who resell them at retail to the Consumers. But they all have this in common, that they *buy in order to resell*, and that their first purchases constitute an advance which is returned to them only in the course of time. It has to be returned to them, as in the case of the advances of the Entrepreneurs in Agriculture and manufacture, not only in its entirety within a certain period in order to be reinvested in new purchases, but also (1) with a profit equal to the revenue they could acquire with their capital without any labour; and (2) with the wages and the price of their labour, their risks, and their industry. Without the assurance of this return and these indispensable profits, no Merchant would undertake Commerce, and no one could continue in it: it is from this point of view that he regulates his behaviour in making his purchases, when he calculates the quantity and the price of the things which he can expect to sell in a certain time. The Retailer learns

157

by experience, and by the success of limited trials undertaken with caution, what is the approximate quantity of the needs of the Consumers he is in a position to supply. The trader, from his Correspondence, acquires knowledge of the abundance or scarcity and the price of commodities in the different Regions to which he extends his Commerce: he directs his speculative activities accordingly, sending the commodities from the place where they are at a low price to those where they are selling at a higher one; it being understood, of course, that the costs of Carriage enter into the calculation of the advances which have to be returned to him.

Since Commerce is necessary, and since it is impossible to undertake any commerce without advances which are proportionate to its extent, we have here another employment of movable wealth, a new use which the possessor of a mass of values put into reserve and accumulated, of a sum of money, in a word of *a capital*, can put it to in order to procure his subsistence and to increase, if possible, his wealth.

LXVIII

True idea of the circulation of money.

We see, from what has just been said, how the cultivation of the land, manufactures of all kinds, and all the branches of commerce depend upon a mass of capitals, or movable accumulated wealth, which, having been first advanced by the Entrepreneurs in each of these different classes of work, must return to them every year with a regular profit; that is, the capital to be reinvested and newly advanced in the continuation of the same enterprises, and the profit to provide for the more or less comfortable subsistence of the Entrepreneurs. It is this continual advance and return of capitals which constitutes *what ought to be called the circulation of money*; that useful and productive circulation which enlivens all the work of society, which maintains movement and life in the body politic, and which is with good reason compared to the circulation of blood in the animal body. For if, through any disarrangement, whatever it may be, in the order of the expenditure of the different classes of society, the Entrepreneurs cease to get back their advances together with the profit which they have a right to expect from them, it is obvious that they will be obliged to reduce their enterprises; that the amount of labour, the amount of consumption of the fruits of the earth, and the amount of production and of revenue will be reduced in like measure; that poverty will take the place of wealth, and that ordinary Workmen, ceasing to find employment, will sink into the most extreme destitution.

LXIX

All enterprises, above all those in manufacture and commerce, must have been very limited before the introduction of gold and silver into commerce.

It is hardly necessary to note that enterprises of all kinds, but especially those in manufacture and even more those in commerce, must have been very limited before the introduction of gold and silver into commerce, since it was almost impossible to accumulate large capitals, and even more difficult to multiply and divide payments as much as is necessary to facilitate and increase exchanges to the extent required by a thriving commerce and circulation. The cultivation of the land alone could maintain itself to some extent, because live-stock constitute the principal object of the advances which it requires; moreover, it is probable that there was then no agricultural Entrepreneur other than the Proprietor. As to the arts of all kinds, they must have languished very greatly before the introduction of money. They were limited to the crudest kinds of work, for which the Proprietors made the advances by feeding the Workmen and providing them with materials, or which they caused to be carried on at home by their Servants.

LXX

Capitals being as necessary to all enterprises as labour and industry, the industrious man willingly shares the profits of his enterprise with the Capitalist who supplies him with the funds he needs.

Since capitals are the indispensable basis of every remunerative enterprise, and since with money one can set up agricultural workshops, establish factories, or found a commercial undertaking, the profits from which when frugally accumulated and put into reserve become new capitals; since, in a word, money is the principal means of attracting money, those who are industrious and like work but have no capital at all, or who do not have enough for the enterprises which they want to establish, have no difficulty in deciding to give up to the Possessors of capitals or money who are willing to entrust them with it, a portion of the profits which they expect to get in over and above the return of their advances.

LXXI

Fifth employment of capitals : the loan at interest. Nature of the loan.

The possessors of money balance the risk which their capital may run if the enterprise should not succeed, against the advantage of enjoying a regular profit without any labour; and they are guided by this in demanding a greater or smaller amount of profit or interest on their money, or in agreeing to lend it at the interest which is offered to them by the Borrower. Here is another outlet which is open to the Possessor of money, the loan at interest, or trade in money. For there must be no mistake about it: the loan at interest is nothing at all but a trading transaction in which the Lender is a man who sells the use of his money, and the Borrower a man who buys it; in exactly the same way as the Proprietor of a piece of land and a Farmer respectively sell and buy the use of an estate which is being leased. This is perfectly expressed by the name which the Latins gave to the interest on loaned money – *usura pecuniae*, words of which the French translation has become odious in consequence of the false ideas which have been adopted about interest on money.

LXXII

False ideas about the loan at interest.

The price of the loan is by no means based, as might be imagined, on the profit the Borrower expects to make with the capital of which he buys the use. This price is determined, like the price of all commodities, by the haggling which takes place between the seller and the buyer, by the balance of supply and demand. People borrow with every kind of design and for every kind of motive. One man borrows to establish an enterprise which will make his fortune, another to buy a piece of land, one to pay a gaming debt, one to make up for the loss of his revenue of which some accident has deprived him, and one to enable himself to live until he is able to earn something by his labour; but all these motives which influence the borrower are a matter of complete indifference to the lender. The latter is concerned about two things only, the interest which he will receive, and the security of his capital. He does not worry about the use which the borrower will make of it, any more than a merchant concerns himself about the use which the purchaser will make of the commodities he sells to him.

Errors of the Schoolmen refuted.

It is because they have not seen the loan at interest in its true light that certain moralists, more inflexible than enlightened, have sought to have it looked upon as a crime. The scholastic Theologians concluded, from the fact that money produces nothing by itself, that it was unjust to demand interest for money put out on loan. Full of their preconceptions, they fancied that their doctrine was sanctioned by this passage from the Gospel: *mutuum date nihil inde sperantes.* Those Theologians who adopted more reasonable principles on the subject of interest were subjected to the sharpest reproaches from the Writers who belonged to the opposite party.

Nevertheless it needs only a little reflection to appreciate the shallowness of the pretexts which have been used to condemn the loan at interest. The loan is a reciprocal contract, which is freely entered into by the two parties and which they make only because it is advantageous to them. It is obvious that if the lender finds an advantage in receiving a payment for the hire of his money, the borrower is equally interested in finding the money of which he stands in need, as is shown by the fact that he makes up his mind to borrow this money and to pay for the hire of it. But in accordance with what principle can one conceive of any element of crime in a contract which is advantageous to the two parties, with which both are content, and which certainly does not injure anyone else? To say that the lender takes unfair advantage of the borrower's need for money in order to demand interest on it is to speak as absurdly as if one should say that a baker who demands money for the bread that he sells takes unfair advantage of the purchaser's need for it. If in the latter case the money is the equivalent of the bread which the purchaser receives, the money which the borrower receives today is equally the equivalent of the capital and the interest which he promises to return at the end of a certain time:

for it is in fact an advantage to the borrower to have during this interval the money of which he stands in need, and it is a disadvantage to the lender to be deprived of it. This disadvantage is appraisable, and it is appraised: the *interest* is its price. This price is bound to be still higher if the lender runs the risk of losing his capital through the insolvency of the borrower. The bargain, therefore, is a perfectly equal one on each side, and is consequently justifiable. Money considered as a physical substance, as a mass of metal, produces nothing; but money employed as advances in agricultural, manufacturing, and commercial enterprises procures a certain profit; with money one can acquire a piece of land and procure a revenue for oneself: thus the person who lends his money does not simply give up the barren possession of that money, but deprives himself of the profit or revenue which he could have procured for himself, and the interest which compensates him for this deprivation cannot be regarded as unjust. The Schoolmen, forced to defer to these considerations, allowed that interest on money could be taken provided that the capital was alienated, that is, provided that the lender renounced the right to demand the repayment of his money at a certain time, and left the borrower free to keep it as long as he wished while simply paying interest on it. The reason put forward for their toleration of this was that then the interest was no longer something derived from the lending-out of a sum of money: it was an annuity which one purchased with a sum of money, just as one purchased a piece of land. This was a petty subterfuge to which they had recourse in order that they might concede the absolute necessity of lending operations in the course of the affairs of Society, without frankly acknowledging the falsity of the principles according to which they had condemned them. But this stipulation about the alienation of capital is by no means an advantage to the borrower, who still remains charged with the debt until he has repaid this capital, and whose property is always liable as security for this capital. It is even a positive disadvantage, in that he finds it more difficult to borrow money when he needs it; for a man who would willingly agree to lend for a year or two a sum of money with which he plans to buy a piece of land, would not be willing to lend it for an indefinite period. Moreover, if one is allowed to sell one's money in return for a perpetual annuity, why should one not be allowed to let it out for a certain number of years, in return for an annuity which will continue only for that number of years? If an annuity of *1,000 francs* a year is the equivalent of a sum of *20,000 francs* to the man who keeps that sum in perpetuity, 1,000 francs will be the equivalent each year of the possession of that sum during a year.

LXXIV

True foundation of the interest on money.

A man, then, is as justified in letting out his money as he is in selling it; and the possessor of money may do either one or the other, not only because the money is the equivalent of a revenue and a means for procuring him a revenue, not only because the lender loses during the term of the loan the revenue which he would have been able to procure, not only because he risks his capital, not only because the borrower may employ it in advantageous purchases or in enterprises from which he will derive large profits: the Proprietor of money may justifiably draw interest on it in accordance with a principle which is more general and more decisive. Even if none of the foregoing were the case, he would nevertheless be justified in demanding interest on the loan, simply for the reason that his money is his own. Since it is his own, he is free to keep it; there is no obligation at all upon him to lend it out: if then he does lend it out, he may attach to his loan whatever condition he wishes. In doing this he does no wrong to the borrower, since the latter acquiesces in the condition, and has no kind of right to the sum lent. The profit that a man may obtain with the money is no doubt one of the commonest motives influencing the borrower to borrow at interest; it is one of the sources of the ease with which he finds himself able to pay this interest, but this is not at all what gives a right to the lender to demand it; for that, it is enough that his money is his own, and this right is inseparable from property. He who buys bread does so in order to feed himself; but the right which the Baker has to demand a price for it is quite independent of this use of the bread: it is the same right which he would have to sell him stones – a right founded solely upon the fact that since the bread is his own, nobody has a right to oblige him to give it away for nothing.

LXXV

Reply to an objection.

This reflection enables us to appreciate how false is the application made by the rigorists of the passage *Mutuum date, nihil inde sperantes* (lend, not hoping for gain), and how far it departs from the meaning of the Gospel. This passage is clear when it is understood, as it is by moderate and reasonable Theologians, as a precept of charity. All men ought to come to one another's assistance: a wealthy man who saw his fellow-creature in want and sold him his assistance instead of relieving his distress would be failing alike in the duties of Christianity and in those of humanity. In circumstances such as these charity does not simply prescribe lending without interest: it commands us to lend, and even to give, if necessary. To make of this precept of charity a precept of rigorous justice is equally repugnant to reason and to the meaning of the text. Those whom I am attacking here do not claim that it is a duty of justice to lend one's money; they must therefore agree that the first words of the passage, *mutuum date*, embody no more than a principle of charity. Why then, I ask, do they say that the close of the passage should be interpreted as a duty of justice? What, shall the lending itself not be a rigorous precept, but its accessory, the condition of the loan, be made into one? If so, men would in effect be being told this: 'You are free to lend or not to lend; but, if you lend, take care that you do not accept any interest on your money; even if a Merchant should ask a loan from you for an enterprise from which he expects to make large profits, it would be a crime for you to take the interest which he offers you; it is absolutely necessary that you should either lend to him gratuitously or not lend to him at all. You have indeed one means of making interest justifiable – you can lend your capital for an indefinite period and renounce the right to demand its repayment, which your debtor may make when he wishes or when he can. If you find that this has drawbacks on the grounds of security, or if you foresee that you are going to need your money in a certain number of years, the only course you can take is not to lend: it is better to allow this Merchant to miss the most precious opportunity than to commit a sin in order to help him to take advantage of it.' That is what has been discovered in these five words, *mutuum date, nihil inde sperantes*, when they have been interpreted with the preconceptions created by a false metaphysics. Everyone who reads this text without prejudice will see what it really means: '*As men, as Christians, you are all brothers and all friends: act towards one another as brothers and as friends; help one another in your necessities; let your purses be open to one another, and do not sell the assistance which you mutually owe to one another by demanding interest on a loan which charity makes it your duty to give.*' That is the true meaning of the passage in question. The obligation to lend without interest and the obligation to lend are clearly related to one another: they are of the same order, and both of them set forth a duty of charity and not a precept of rigorous justice applicable to all cases in which lending may take place.

LXXVI

The rate of interest ought to be fixed, like the prices of all commodities, by nothing but the course of trade alone.

I have already said that the price of borrowed money is regulated, like that of all other commodities, by the balance of supply and demand: thus, when there is a large number of borrowers who are in need of money, interest on money becomes higher; when there is a large number of possessors of money who are offering to lend it, interest falls. Thus it is once again a mistake to believe that interest on money in commerce ought to be fixed by the laws of Princes. It is a current price, fixed like that of all other commodities. This price varies a little according to the greater or smaller degree of security which the lender has that he will not lose his capital; but with equal security it must rise or fall in proportion to the abundance and the need; and the law ought no more to fix the rate of interest on money than it ought to regulate the price of any of the other commodities which are in circulation in commerce.

LXXVII

Money in commerce has two distinct valuations : one expresses the quantity of money which is given to obtain different kinds of commodities ; the other expresses the relation which a sum of money bears to the interest which it yields according to the course of trade.

It will appear from this explanation of the manner in which money is sold or let out for an annual interest that there are two ways of valuing money in commerce. In purchases and sales, a certain weight of money represents a certain quantity of values or of commodities of all kinds: for example, an ounce of silver is the equivalent of a certain quantity of corn, or of a certain number of days' labour. In lending, and in trade in money, a capital is the equivalent of an annual payment equal to a fixed proportion of this capital; and conversely an annual payment represents a capital equal to the amount of this annual payment multiplied a certain number of times, according to whether interest is at a higher or lower number of years' purchase.

LXXVIII

These two valuations are independent of one another, and are regulated by quite different principles.

These two different appraisals have much less connection and depend much less upon one another than one would at first sight be tempted to believe. Money may be very plentiful in everyday commerce, it may have very little value there, and it may correspond to a very small quantity of commodities, while at the same time interest on money may be at a very high level.

Let us assume that with *one million ounces of silver* at present circulating in commerce, *one ounce of silver* is given on the market for a measure of corn. Let us now assume that there is brought into the State, by some means or other, *a second million* ounces of silver, and that this increase is distributed to everyone in the same proportion as the first million, so that the man who formerly had two ounces of silver now has four. The money, considered as a mass of metal, will certainly diminish in price, or, what amounts to the same thing, commodities will be paid for at a dearer price; and, in order to obtain the measure of corn which was formerly bought for one ounce of silver, it will be necessary to give a good deal more silver – perhaps *two ounces* instead of *one*. But it will by no means follow from this that interest on money will fall, if all this money is brought to the market and employed in the current expenditure of those who possess it, as we have assumed that the first million ounces of silver were; for interest on money falls only when there is more money to lend, relative to the needs of borrowers, than there was before. But the money which people bring to the market is not for lending at all; it is the money which is put into reserve, the accumulated capitals, that are lent; and so far from the increase in the money in the market, or the lowering of its price relative to the commodities entering into everyday commerce, infallibly and as a direct consequence leading to a fall in the interest on money, it may on the contrary happen that the very cause which increases the amount of money in the market, and which increases the prices of other commodities by lowering the price of money, is precisely the cause which increases the price of money, or the rate of interest.

Indeed, let us assume for a moment that all the wealthy men in a nation, instead of saving out of their revenues or their annual profits, should spend the whole of them; that, not content with spending the whole of their revenue, they should spend their capital; that a man who has 100,000 francs in money, instead of employing it in a profitable manner or lending it out, should consume it bit by bit in frivolous expenditure: it is clear that on the one hand there will be more money employed in current purchases, for the satisfaction of the needs or whims of each individual, and that consequently its price will fall; while on the other hand there will certainly be much less money available for lending; and, since many people will be ruined, there will probably also be more borrowers. Interest on money will therefore rise, while money will become more plentiful in the market and will fall in price there, and precisely for the same reason.

We shall cease to be surprised at this apparent inconsistency if we remember that the money which is offered in the market to obtain corn is that which is spent every day to satisfy one's needs, and that the money which is offered on loan is precisely that which is held back from one's everyday expenditure to be put into reserve and used to create capitals.

LXXIX

In the valuation of money relative to commodities, it is the money considered as metal which is the subject of the appraisal. In the valuation of the number of years' purchase of money, it is the use of the money during a given period which is the subject of the appraisal.

In the market, a measure of corn is balanced against a certain weight of silver; it is a quantity of silver which is purchased with the commodity; it is this quantity which is appraised, and which is compared with the different values of other things. In the loan at interest, the subject of the appraisal is the use of a certain quantity of values during a certain period. It is no longer a mass of silver which is compared with a mass of corn; it is now a mass of values which is compared with a determinate proportion of itself, the latter becoming the price of the use of this mass during a certain period. Whether *20,000 ounces of silver* are the equivalent in the market of *20,000 measures of corn*, or only of *10,000*, the use of these 20,000 ounces of silver during one year will in the loan market be worth not less than a *twentieth* part of the principal sum, or *1,000 ounces of silver*, if interest is at *twenty years' purchase*.

LXXX

The rate of interest depends directly upon the relation between the demand of the borrowers and the supply of the lenders, and this relation depends mainly upon the quantity of movable wealth which is accumulated as a result of saving out of revenues and annual products in order to create capitals, whether these capitals exist in the form of money or of any other kind of effects which have a value in commerce.

The price of silver in the market is relative only to the quantity of this metal employed in current exchanges; but the rate of interest is relative to the quantity of values accumulated and put into reserve in order to create capitals. It is immaterial whether these values are in the form of the money metal or of other effects, provided that these effects are easily convertible into money. It is far from being the case that the mass of the monetary metal which exists in a State is as large as the sum of values which is lent at interest in the course of a year: but all the capitals in the form of equipment, commodities, implements, and live-stock take the place of this money and represent it. A paper signed by a man who is well known to have effects worth *100,000 francs*, and who promises to pay *100,000 francs* at such and such a date, passes up to that date for 100,000 francs: all the capitals of the man who has signed this note answer for the payment, whatever the nature of the effects which he has in his possession, provided that they have a value of *100,000 francs*. Thus it is not the quantity of money existing in the form of metal which causes interest on money to rise or fall, or which brings into commerce a greater supply of money to lend; it is solely the sum of capitals to be found in commerce, that is, the current sum of movable values of all kinds, accumulated and saved bit by bit out of revenues and profits, in order to be employed to obtain for their possessor new revenues and new profits. It is these accumulated savings which are offered to borrowers; and the more there are of them the lower will interest on money be, at any rate if the number of borrowers is not increased in proportion.

LXXXI

The spirit of economy in a nation continually increases the sum of capitals; luxury continually tends to destroy them.

The spirit of economy in a nation continually tends to increase the sum of its capitals, to increase the number of lenders, and to diminish the number of borrowers. The habit of luxury has exactly the opposite effect; and from what has already been said about the use of capitals in all the enterprises of agriculture, industry, or commerce one can judge whether luxury enriches a nation or whether it impoverishes it.

LXXXII

The fall in interest proves that in general economy has prevailed over luxury in Europe.

Since for several centuries interest on money has continually been diminishing in Europe, it must be concluded that the spirit of economy has been more general than the spirit of luxury. It is only men who are already wealthy who give themselves up to luxury; and, among the wealthy, all those who are sensible limit themselves to spending their revenue, and take great care not to break into their capitals. Those who wish to become wealthy are much more numerous in a nation than those who are already wealthy; but in the present state of things, when all the land is occupied, there is only one way to become wealthy, and that is to possess or to obtain for oneself, by whatever means, a revenue or annual profit over and above what is absolutely necessary for one's subsistence, and to put this surplus into reserve each year in order to create a capital, by means of which one may obtain an increase in revenue or annual profit, which may again be saved and converted into capital. Thus there are large numbers of men who are interested in and engaged in amassing capitals.

LXXXIII

Recapitulation of the five different methods of employing capitals.

I have listed five different methods of employing capitals, or of investing them profitably.

The first is to buy a landed estate which brings in a certain revenue.

The second is to invest one's money in agricultural enterprises, by taking a lease of land, the produce of which ought to yield, over and above the rent, the interest on the advances and the reward for the labour of the man who devotes both his wealth and his trouble to its cultivation.

The third is to invest one's capital in industrial or manufacturing enterprises.

The fourth is to invest it in commercial enterprises.

And the fifth is to lend it to those who are in need of it, at an annual interest.

LXXXIV

Influence upon one another of the different employments of money.

It is obvious that the annual products which can be derived from capitals invested in these different employments are mutually limited by one another, and that all are relative to the existing rate of interest on money.

LXXXV

Money invested in land is bound to bring in least.

The man who invests his money in the purchase of an estate which is let out to a completely solvent Farmer obtains for himself a revenue whose receipt involves him in very little trouble, and which he can spend in the most agreeable manner by giving free rein to all his tastes. He has in addition the advantage of acquiring that form of property the possession of which above all others is the most assured against every kind of accident. Thus one must pay a higher price for a given revenue obtained from land, or be content with a smaller revenue from the investment of a given capital.

LXXXVI

*Money placed on loan is bound to bring in a little more than the revenue of
land purchased with an equal capital.*

The man who lends his money at interest enjoys it even more peaceably
and freely than the possessor of land; but the insolvency of his debtor is
capable of bringing about the loss of his capital. Thus he will not be
content with an interest equal to the revenue of the land which he could
buy with the same capital. Interest on money placed on loan must therefore be higher than the revenue from an estate purchased with the same
capital; for if the lender found an estate for sale with a revenue equal to
the interest, he would prefer that employment of his money.

LXXXVII

*Money invested in agricultural, manufacturing, and commercial enterprises is
bound to bring in more than the interest on money placed on loan.*

For a similar reason, money employed in agriculture, industry, and commerce ought to bring in a profit which is greater than the revenue of
the same capital when employed in the purchase of land, or the interest
on the same amount of money placed on loan; for since these employments require, besides the capital which is advanced, a great deal of
trouble and labour, if they were not more remunerative it would be much
better to obtain a revenue of equal amount which could be enjoyed without having to do anything. Thus it is necessary that the entrepreneur,
over and above the interest on his capital, should every year draw a profit
which compensates him for his trouble, his labour, his talent, and his
risks, and which in addition provides him with the means to make good
the annual wear and tear of his advances, which he is obliged from the
very first to convert into effects which are susceptible to deterioration,
and which are moreover exposed to all kinds of accidents.

LXXXVIII

Nevertheless the products of these different employments mutually limit one another, and in spite of their inequality are kept in a kind of equilibrium.

Thus the different employments of capitals bring in very unequal products; but this inequality does not prevent their having a reciprocal influence on one another, nor the establishment of a kind of equilibrium between them, like that between two liquids of unequal gravity which come into contact with one another at the base of an inverted siphon whose two branches they occupy: they will not be on a level, but the height of one cannot increase without the other also rising in the opposite branch.

Let us assume that a very large number of proprietors of estates suddenly want to sell them. It is obvious that the price of land will fall, and that one will be able to acquire a greater revenue by the expenditure of a smaller sum. This cannot happen without interest on money becoming higher, for the possessors of money will prefer to buy land rather than to lend at an interest which is no higher than the revenue of the land which they could purchase. If, then, borrowers want to have money, they will be obliged to pay a higher price for it. If interest on money becomes higher, people will prefer to lend it out rather than to turn it to account in a more troublesome and risky manner in agricultural, industrial, and commercial enterprises; and only those enterprises will be embarked upon which bring in, over and above the wages of the labour, a profit much greater than the rate of interest on money placed on loan. In a word, as soon as the profits resulting from one employment of money, whatever it may be, increase or diminish, capitals either turn in its direction and are withdrawn from the other employments, or are withdrawn from it and turn in the direction of the other employments; and this necessarily alters in each of these employments the ratio between the capital and the annual product. In general, money converted into landed property brings in less than money placed on loan, and money placed on loan brings in less than money employed in enterprises involving work; but whatever the manner in which money is employed, its product cannot increase or diminish without all the other employments experiencing a proportionate increase or diminution.

LXXXIX

The current interest on money is the thermometer by which one may judge of the abundance or scarcity of capitals; it is the measure of the extent to which a Nation can carry its agricultural, manufacturing, and commercial enterprises.

The current interest on money placed on loan can thus be regarded as a kind of thermometer of the abundance or scarcity of capitals in a Nation, and of the extent of the enterprises of all kinds in which it may engage. It is obvious that the lower the interest on money is, the greater will be the value of land. A man who has an annual income of 50,000 livres, when land is sold at only twenty years' purchase, owns wealth to the value of only one million, whereas he owns two millions if land is sold at forty years' purchase. If interest is at five per cent, all uncleared land whose product would not bring in five per cent, over and above the replacement of the advances and compensation for the Cultivator's trouble, will remain uncultivated. No manufacturing or commercial enterprise which will not bring in five per cent, over and above the wages and the equivalent of the trouble and risks of the Entrepreneur, will exist. If there is a neighbouring Nation in which interest is at only two per cent, then not only will it carry on all the trade from which the Nation where interest is at five per cent finds itself excluded, but in addition, since its manufacturers and merchants are able to content themselves with a lower profit, they will put their commodities on all the markets at a lower price, and attract to themselves an almost exclusive trade in all those goods in respect of which neither particular circumstances nor excessive costs of carriage are able to keep the trade in the hands of the nation where money is at five per cent.

XC

Influence of the rate of interest on money on all remunerative enterprises.

The rate of interest may be regarded as a kind of water-level, below which all labour, all cultivation, all industry, and all commerce come to an end. It is like a sea spread over a vast region: the summits of the mountains rise above the waters, and form fertile and cultivated islands. If this sea should happen to roll back, to the extent that its level falls the land on the slopes is revealed, and then the plains and the valleys, and they are covered with every kind of produce. It is enough that the water should rise or fall by a foot to inundate huge tracts or open them up for cultivation. It is the abundance of capitals which gives life to all enterprises; and a low rate of interest on money is at one and the same time the effect and the sign of an abundance of capitals.

XCI

The total Wealth of a nation is composed of (1) the net revenue of all the landed property multiplied by the rate at which land is sold; and (2) the sum of all the movable wealth which exists in the nation.

Landed estates are the equivalent of a capital equal to their annual revenue multiplied by the number of years' purchase at which land is currently sold. Thus if we add up the revenue of all the land, that is, the net revenue which it yields to the proprietors and to all those who share in its ownership, such as the Seigneur who collects the dues, the Priest who collects the tithes, and the Sovereign who collects the taxes; if, I say, we add up all these sums, and multiply them by the rate at which land is sold, we shall have the total of the Nation's wealth in the form of landed property. To obtain the grand total of a Nation's wealth, we must also include its movable wealth, consisting of the sum of the capitals which are employed in all the agricultural, industrial, and commercial enterprises, and which never come out of them, since all the advances in every kind of enterprise have to return continually to the entrepreneurs in order to be continually reinvested in the enterprise, which, without this, could not be continued. It would be a very gross error to confuse the immense mass of this movable wealth with the mass of money which exists in a State; the latter is a very small thing in comparison. To be convinced of this, it is enough to remember the immense quantity of live-stock, implements, and seed which constitute the advances of Agriculture; the materials, tools, equipment, and commodities of all kinds which fill the workrooms, shops, and warehouses of every Manufacturer, every Merchant, and every Trader; and one will then realise that in the grand total of the wealth, both landed and movable, of a Nation, money in the form of specie makes only a very small part. But since all forms of wealth are continually exchangeable with money, they all represent money, and money represents them all.

174

XCII

The amount of capitals on loan could not be included in this total without double counting.

In the calculation of the Nation's wealth we must not include the amount of capitals on loan; for these capitals can have been lent only to proprietors of land, or to entrepreneurs who turn them to account in their enterprises, since it is only these two kinds of people who can answer for a capital and pay the interest. A sum of money lent to a person who had neither estate nor industry would be a dead capital, not one in active use. If the proprietor of an estate of 400,000 francs borrows 100,000 on it, his property is charged with an annual payment which diminishes his revenue accordingly; and, if he sold his property, out of the 400,000 francs which he received 100,000 would belong to the lender. Thus if the capital of the lender were included in the calculation of the existing wealth, in addition to the equivalent part of the value of the land, this would represent double counting. The land is always worth 400,000 francs: and when the proprietor borrows 100,000 francs, that does not make its value 500,000 francs. It merely brings it about that out of the 400,000 francs 100,000 belong to the lender, and that there no longer belong to the borrower any more than 300,000.

The same double counting would occur if we included in the calculation of the total sum of capitals the money lent to an entrepreneur for employment as the advances of his enterprise; for this loan does not increase the sum total of the advances necessary for the enterprise. It merely brings it about that this sum, and the portion of the profits which represents interest on it, belong to the lender. Whether a merchant employs 10,000 francs of his own property in his trade and takes the whole profit from it, or whether he has borrowed these 10,000 francs from another to whom he pays interest, contenting himself with the surplus profit and the wages of his industry, there are never more than 10,000 francs.

But although the capital corresponding to the interest on loaned money cannot without double counting be included in the calculation of the wealth of a nation, we ought to include in it all the other items of movable property which, although they originally constituted an object of expenditure and do not yield any profit, nevertheless by reason of their durability become a true capital which is continually accumulating and

175

which, since it can if necessary be exchanged for money, constitutes as it were a reserve fund which may enter into commerce, and make up, when one pleases, for the loss of other capitals. Such are furnishings of all kinds, jewels, plate, paintings, statues, and ready money locked up in the chests of misers: all these things have a value, and the total of all these values may in a wealthy nation be considerable. But whether it is considerable or not, it is always true that it ought to be added to the sum of the values of landed property, and to that of the advances circulating in enterprises of all kinds, in order to make up the grand total of the wealth of a nation. However, it is hardly necessary to say that although we may very well define, as we have just done, in what the total wealth of a nation consists, it is in all probability impossible to find out how much it actually amounts to, at any rate so long as we cannot find some rule by which to determine the proportion which the total commerce of a nation bears to the revenue of its land – something which is feasible, perhaps, but which has not yet been done in such a way as to dispel all doubts.

XCIII

In which of the three classes of Society should one include the capitalist lenders of money?

Let us now see how what we have just said about the different methods of employing capitals squares with what we previously laid down about the division of all the members of Society into three classes – the productive class, or that of agriculturists, the industrial or commercial class, and the disposable class, or that of proprietors.

XCIV

The capitalist lender of money, so far as his person is concerned, belongs to the disposable class.

We have seen that every wealthy man is necessarily the possessor either of a capital in the form of movable wealth, or of an estate equivalent to a capital. Every landed estate is the equivalent of a capital: thus every proprietor is a capitalist, but every capitalist is not the proprietor of a landed estate; and the possessor of a movable capital can choose either to

THE FORMATION AND THE DISTRIBUTION OF WEALTH

employ it in acquiring an estate or to turn it to account in the enterprises of the agricultural class or the industrial class. The capitalist who has become an agricultural or industrial entrepreneur is no more disposable, either as regards himself or his profits, than the ordinary workman in these two classes; both assigned are to the continuation of their enterprises. The capitalist who confines himself to being only a lender of money lends either to a proprietor or to an entrepreneur. If he lends to a proprietor, he would appear to belong to the class of proprietors; he becomes a co-partner in the property; the revenue of the land is pledged for the payment of the interest on his debt; the value of the estate is pledged to provide security for his capital up to the amount due. If the lender of money has lent to an entrepreneur, it is certain that in his person he belongs to the disposable class; but his capital is sunk in the advances of the enterprise, and cannot be withdrawn from it without injuring the enterprise, unless it is replaced by a capital of equal value.

XCV

The interest drawn by the lender of money is disposable, so far as the use which he may make of it is concerned.

It is true that the interest which he draws from this capital appears to be disposable, since the entrepreneur and the enterprise can do without it; it would also appear that we could conclude from this that in the profits of the two industrious classes employed either in cultivation or in industry there is a disposable portion, namely that which corresponds to the interest on the advances calculated according to the current rate of interest on money placed on loan; and it would also appear that this conclusion is in conflict with what we have said – that it is only the class of proprietors which has a revenue properly so-called, a disposable revenue, and that all the members of the other two classes have only wages or profits. This point needs to be cleared up. If we consider the 1,000 crowns drawn annually by a man who has lent 60,000 francs to a merchant in relation to the use which he may make of them, we can have no doubt that they are perfectly disposable, since the enterprise can do without them.

XCVI

Interest on money is not disposable in this sense, that the State can without any disadvantage appropriate part of it for its own needs.

But it does not follow that they are disposable in the sense that the State can with impunity appropriate a portion of them for public needs. These 1,000 crowns are not a return which cultivation or commerce furnishes gratuitously to the man who has made the advances; they are the price and the condition of this advance, without which the enterprise could not carry on. If this return is diminished, the capitalist will withdraw his money and the enterprise will come to an end. Thus this return ought to be inviolable and enjoy complete immunity, because it is the price of an advance made to the enterprise, without which the enterprise could not carry on. To interfere with it would be to increase the price of advances for all enterprises, and thus to diminish the enterprises themselves – i.e., agriculture, industry, and commerce.

This reply should lead us to conclude that if we have said that the capitalist who lends to a proprietor *would appear* to belong to the class of proprietors, this *appearance* has something equivocal about it which needs to be unravelled. In fact the exact truth is that the interest on his money is no more disposable, i.e., no more capable of being encroached upon, than that on money lent to agricultural and commercial entrepreneurs. This interest is equally the price of a free agreement, and one can no more encroach upon it without bringing about a deterioration or change in the price at which money is lent: for it matters little to whom the loan has been made; if the price of the loan changes and increases for the proprietor, it will also change and increase for the cultivator, the manufacturer, and the merchant. In a word, the capitalist lender of money ought to be considered as one who trades in a commodity which is absolutely necessary for the production of wealth, and which cannot be at too low a price. It is as unreasonable to burden this trade with a tax as to put a tax on the dung which serves to manure the land. From this we may conclude that the lender of money belongs properly to the disposable class, as regards his person, because he has nothing to do; but not as regards the nature of his wealth, whether the interest on his money is paid by the proprietor of land out of a portion of his revenue, or whether it is paid by an entrepreneur out of that part of his profits which is earmarked for the interest on the advances.

XCVII

Objection.

It will no doubt be replied that the capitalist may indifferently either lend his money or employ it in acquiring land; that in either case he receives only a price which is the equivalent of his money; and that in whatever way he may employ it he ought none the less to contribute towards public expenditure.

XCVIII

Reply to the objection.

I would reply, in the first place, that it is true that when the capitalist has bought an estate the revenue is the equivalent for him of what he would have got from his money if he had lent it; but there is this essential difference for the State, that the price he gives for his land contributes nothing to the revenue it produces; it would not have yielded less revenue if he had not bought it: this revenue, as I have explained, is what the land gives over and above the wages of the cultivators, their profits, and the interest on the advances. It is not the same with the interest on a loan: it is the very condition of the loan, the price of the advance, without which neither the revenue nor the profits which serve to pay it would exist.

I would also reply, in the second place, that if land alone were burdened with taxes to meet public expenditure, as soon as these taxes were determined the capitalist who bought the land would not reckon in the interest on his money that part of the revenue earmarked for the taxes, just as a man who buys an estate today does not buy the tithe which the Priest receives, but rather the revenue which remains after this tithe has been deducted.

XCIX

There exists no truly disposable revenue in a State except the net product of land.

We can see from what has been said that interest on money placed on loan is taken either out of the revenue of land or out of the profits of agricultural, industrial, or commercial enterprises. But we have already shown that these profits themselves are only a part of the product of land; that the product of land is divided into two portions; that one is earmarked for the wages of the cultivator, for his profits, and for the return of his advances and the interest on them; and that the other is the share of the proprietor, or the revenue which the proprietor spends at his pleasure, and out of which he contributes to the general expenditure of the State. We have shown that all that the other classes of Society receive is wages and profits, which are paid either by the proprietor out of his revenue, or by the agents of the productive class out of the part which is earmarked for their needs, to satisfy which they are obliged to buy from the industrial class. Whether these profits are distributed in the form of workmen's wages, entrepreneurs' profits, or interest on advances, they do not change their nature, and do not increase at all the total amount of revenue produced by the productive class over and above the price of its labour, in which the industrial class shares only to the extent of the price of its labour.

It still remains true, therefore, that there is no revenue except the net product of land, and that all other annual profit is either paid out of the revenue, or forms part of the expenditure which serves to produce the revenue.

C

The land has also provided the whole amount of movable wealth or capitals in existence, and these are formed only as the result of a portion of its product being put into reserve each year.

Not only is it the case that there neither exists nor can exist any revenue other than the net product of the land, but it is also the land which has provided all the capitals which constitute the totality of all the advances in cultivation and commerce. Land offered, without being cultivated, the first rude advances which were indispensable for the first labours; all the rest is the accumulated fruit of the economy of the centuries which have followed one another since man began to cultivate the land. This economy has no doubt been exercised not only in relation to the revenues of the proprietors but also in relation to the profits of all the members of the industrious classes. It is even true in general that although the proprietors have a greater surplus they save less, because, having more leisure, they have more desires and more passions; they regard themselves as being more assured of their fortunes; they think more about enjoying them agreeably than about increasing them; luxury is their lot. The wage-earners and above all the entrepreneurs of the other classes, who receive profits proportionate to their advances, their talents, and their activity, although they have no revenue at all properly so called, have a surplus over and above their subsistence; and almost all of them, devoting themselves exclusively to their enterprises, occupied in increasing their fortunes, and diverted by their work from costly amusements and passions, save the whole of their surplus in order to reinvest it in their enterprises and increase it. The majority of agricultural entrepreneurs borrow little, and scarcely any of them seek to turn to account anything but their own funds. The entrepreneurs in other fields of activity, who want to consolidate their fortunes, also try to achieve the same position; and, unless they are very able, those who base their enterprises on borrowed funds run a great risk of failing. But although capitals are formed in part by means of savings from the profits of the industrious classes, yet, as these profits always come from the land – since all are paid either out of the revenue or out of the expenditure which serves to pro-duce the revenue – it is obvious that capitals come from the land just as the revenue does, or rather that they are simply the accumulation of that part of the values produced by the land which the proprietors of the land, or those who share it with them, can put into reserve each year without using it to meet their needs.

CI

Although money is the direct object of saving, and is so to speak the raw material of capitals in the process of their formation, specie constitutes only an almost imperceptible part of the sum total of capitals.

We have seen that money counts for almost nothing in the sum total of existing capitals; but it counts for a great deal in the formation of capitals.

In fact almost all savings are made only in the form of money; it is in the form of money that revenues are returned to proprietors, and that advances and profits are returned to entrepreneurs of all kinds; thus it is money which they save, and the annual increase of capitals comes about in the form of money: but none of the entrepreneurs make any other use of it than to convert it immediately into the different kinds of effects upon which their enterprise depends. Thus this money comes back into circulation, and the greater part of capitals exists only in the form of effects of different kinds, as has already been explained above.

November 1766.

Index

accumulation of capital, 22–3, 145–8, 150–
152, 159, 166, 169, 175, 181–2
advances, 17, 21–2, 26, 31, 34, 37, 39,
119–82 *passim*
agriculture, 9–10, 16–18, 20–5, 31–3, 35–6,
43, 68–9, 75, 91, 119–82 *passim*
Alexander, 50–1, 105–6, 112
America and the American Indians, 5, 10,
30, 42, 47, 66, 71, 88–90, 110, 130, 148,
157
Angoumois, 2, 31, 155
architecture, 50, 58, 103–4, 116
Aristotle, 50, 55, 94
Arminius, 105
astronomy, 12, 47, 50, 58, 90–1, 95–6, 117
Augustine, Saint, 107

Bacon, F., 58, 94
Baillie, J., 29
banking, 15
Becker, C. L., 29
Berkeley, G., 95
Boussuet, J. B., 7, 28–9, 61, 106

Caesars, the, 77
Caillard, M., 39
Caligula, 77
Cantillon, R., 30–1, 33
capital, 14–17, 19, 21–6, 30–1, 33, 36, 119–
182 *passim*
capitalism and capitalists, 20–6, 30–3, 36,
134–82 *passim*
Charlemagne, 54, 56
chemistry, 55, 102, 142
Christianity, 6–7, 29–30, 56, 71, 164
Cicé, Abbé de, 15
Cicero, 51, 53, 106
circulation, 15, 30, 119–82 *passim*
Claudian, 109
Columbia University, 38–40
Columbus, 88
commerce and trade, 9, 11, 15–18, 21–6,
33, 35, 41, 43, 54–6, 58, 67, 69, 73, 76,
92, 104, 115, 119–82 *passim*

competition, 15, 21, 31, 119–82 *passim*
Condillac, E. B. de, 95
Condorcet, Marquis de, 7, 13–14
Confucius, 112
Corneille, P., 88, 109
credit, 15, 125–6
Cyrus, 76

Daire, E., 3
dance, 12, 91
Darius, 50
democracy, 74, 80
Demosthenes, 53, 105, 107, 109
Descartes, R., 58, 94–6, 99
despotism, 47, 72–3, 76–83, 111, 117
diminishing returns, 13, 19, 33
Diodorus Siculus, 89
disposable revenue and classes, 21, 24–6,
127, 176–81
distribution of wealth, 14, 119–82 *passim*
division of labour, 21, 43, 89, 121, 145
Du Pont de Nemours, P.-S., 3–7, 9–10,
13–19, 21, 24–6, 33, 37–8, 61
Dussard, H., 3

education, 43, 72, 79, 88–9
eloquence, 12, 51, 105–7, 115, 117
Encyclopedia, 2, 15, 27
entrepreneurs, 17–27, 30–2, 36, 151–82
passim
equilibrium, 15, 23, 27–8, 44, 49, 74, 172
exchange, 15, 21, 30, 119–82 *passim*

farmers, 36, 119–82 *passim*
Fléchier, E., 106
Francis I, 57
Frénicle de Bessy, 95–6

Galileo, 58, 94
geography, 2, 9, 11, 13, 27, 47, 64, 91, 103
Gournay, Vincent de, 2, 15–16, 27
Graslin, J.-J.-L., 3, 19
Greig, J. Y. T., 13, 18
Groenewegen, P. D., 40
Guido Reni, 113

Cambridge Studies in the History and Theory of Politics

TEXTS

STUDIES